UNDERGROUND TO PALESTINE

I. F. STONE

UNDERGROUND

TO PALESTINE

BONI & GAER

COPYRIGHT, 1946, BY I. F. STONE
PUBLISHED BY BONI & GAER, INC.

15 EAST 40TH STREET
NEW YORK 16, N. Y.

Manufactured in the United States of America
By Parish Press, Inc., New York

 10

To

Those Anonymous Heroes
The *Schlichim* of The *Haganah*

Contents

Contents

"The Germans killed us. The British don't let us live."—Jewish ex-Partisan.

UNDERGROUND TO PALESTINE →

In Explanation

In Explanation

This is a story of personal adventure. I was the first newspaperman to travel the Jewish underground in Europe and to arrive in Palestine on a so-called illegal boat. But this is more than the narrative of a journalistic escapade. I am an American and I am also and inescapably—the world being what it is—a Jew. I was born in the United States. My parents were born in Russia. Had they not emigrated at the turn of the century to America, I might have gone to the gas chambers in Eastern Europe. I might have been a DP, ragged and homeless like those with whom I traveled. I did not go to join them as a tourist in search of the picturesque, nor even as a newspaperman merely in search of a good story, but as a kinsman, fulfilling a moral obligation to my brothers. I wanted in my own way, as a journalist, to provide a picture of their trials and their aspirations in the hope that good people, Jewish and non-Jewish, might be moved to help them.

I have not faked and I have not fictionalized except to hide the names of persons and places. I have not glossed over the unpleasant. My comrades of the voyage would be dishonored by anything less than the truth. I hope that, however inadequately, I may also have provided a record of some value to history. The clandestine exodus of the Jews from postwar Europe is the greatest in the history of a wandering people—greater than the exodus from Egypt or from Spain—because their sufferings under Hitler were greater than any our ancestors ever underwent before. We know comparatively little of the emigration from Egypt or of what went on aboard those tragic ships out of Spain which Columbus may have passed in 1492 on his way to a new world. This narrative may fill a humble gap in the annals of the current emigration. It was a privilege to take part in that emigration. I only wish I had the power to portray what I saw against the background of the world situation today. The plight of the Jews may be a minor affair. But world indifference to that plight is of spiritual significance for the future of us all.

I can only record as a reporter what I saw and heard, traveling with the least fortunate but the bravest of my people.

UNDERGROUND TO PALESTINE

Summons To Adventure

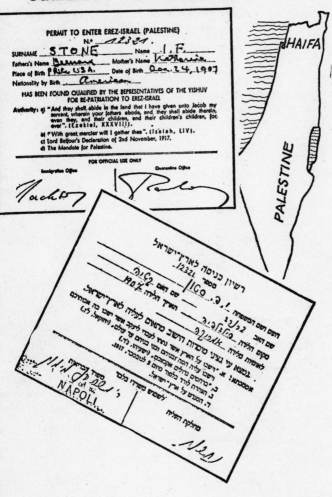

PERMIT TO ENTER EREZ-ISRAEL (PALESTINE)

N° 12321

SURNAME STONE   Name I. F.

Father's Name Bernard   Mother's Name Katharine

Place of Birth Phila, USA.   Date of Birth Dec. 24, 1907

Nationality by Birth American

HAS BEEN FOUND QUALIFIED BY THE REPRESENTATIVES OF THE YISHUV
FOR RE-PATRIATION TO EREZ-ISRAEL

Authority: a) "And they shall abide in the land that I have given unto Jacob my
servant, wherein your fathers abode, and, they shall abide therein,
even they, and their children, and their children's children, for
ever". (Ezekiel, XXXVIII).

b) "With great mercies will I gather thee". (Isaiah, LIV).

c) Lord Balfour's Declaration of 2nd November, 1917.

d) The Mandate for Palestine.

FOR OFFICIAL USE ONLY

Immigration Office   Quarantine Office

HAIFA

PALESTINE

Summons to Adventure

I

I was in the press gallery at Hunter College in the Bronx when the call came. It was April, 1946. The Security Council of the United Nations was in session. The floodlighted scene below me seemed unreal, like the setting for a play—perhaps a play about the fumbling of the peace. Sir Alexander Cadogan, Britain's representative at that horseshoe-shaped council table — a small man, dapper and correct—was making a professionally astringent argument designed to prevent action against Franco. An usher tapped me on the shoulder and said I was wanted on the phone.

3

The interruption was not so irrelevant as it seemed at first. In Sir Alexander's subtle apologetics for a Fascist dictator, I had seen one aspect of the Empire's postwar policy. I was soon to see another. When I picked up the phone in one of the booths in the big press room in the basement, I heard the voice of an American I had met the preceding November in Palestine.

"How would you like to meet some boys who volunteered to serve as seamen for the illegal immigration?" he asked me. Neither of us realized on what a journey that question was to send me.

Of course I was interested. I had reason to believe that the man who phoned me was in close touch with the leaders of the *Haganah,* the Jewish people's militia of Palestine. I had heard many stories of its exploits during the war, when the *Haganah* directed underground rescue work in Hitler Europe. In April, 1946, a year after the liberation, the *Haganah* was back at much the same job, though under altered circumstances. The cruelty of the Nazis had given way to the indifference of the victors; the concentration camps had become DP camps. The Jews in them were still homeless.

Earl Harrison of Philadelphia had returned eight months before from a special tour of these camps to report at the White House, "We seem to be treating the Jews as the Nazis treated them, except that we do not exterminate them." President Truman had asked the British government to open the doors of Palestine to the 100,000 Jews in the displaced persons' camps of Germany and Austria before winter came, but the only result was an

Anglo-American Committee of Inquiry. It was spring and the committee had yet to make its report. A trickle of 1500 a month was entering Palestine legally under the limited immigration quota granted by the British, but the one hope of the rest was still the *Aliyah Beth.*

Aliyah is a Hebrew word which may be translated as "immigration," though its connotations are richer. Literally, the word means an "up-going," as to a high place; its associations are those of the pilgrimage. *Beth* in this context means "second," and distinguishes this immigration from the one allowed by the British. *Aliyah Beth* is the Palestinian term for what the British call the "illegal" immigration; the difference goes deeper than terminology.

This is a subject on which the British do not see eye to eye with the Jews. The Colonial Office looks back to the White Paper of 1939. Under its terms the doors of Palestine should be shut tight against further Jewish immigration. But to the Jews Palestine is still—as in the Bible—*Eretz Israel,* the land of Israel. To them the British are another of those historic vexations like the Assyrians and the Romans. From the Jewish point of view the White Paper is a violation of the Balfour Declaration; the whole affair—the 1917 promise and the 1939 breaking of it—a bit of latter-day presumption. For is it not written, of an older covenant with Abraham, "And He said unto him, I am the Lord that brought thee out of Ur of the Chaldees, to give thee this land to inherit it. . . . Unto thy seed have I given this land"?

This may, indeed, be theological nonsense and stubborn Jewish foolishness. Mr. Bevin and the gentlemen of the

Foreign Office and the Colonial Office may be right in dismissing it as such. But the Jews have been that way for a long time; they were that way long before there was a Britain; unconsciously they feel that way today.

I set all this down at the beginning of my story so that the reader will understand that when my American friend referred to the "illegal immigration" he did so only as a matter of convenience and that when he warned that the visit he suggested must be kept highly confidential, it was not as though he spoke of something shameful or furtive.

I said, "Call me back in fifteen minutes." I phoned my managing editor.

"John," I pleaded, "please let me have the rest of the day off for an expedition of my own. I may never be able to tell you about it, but I know you would agree it was worth while."

He tried to sound exasperated. "Go ahead, Izzy," he told me wearily. "You always were a mysterious guy. I suppose there's no use trying to hold you."

II

When my mysterious friend called back, I arranged to meet him at a railroad station in Manhattan. I took the Lexington Avenue subway downtown. I have never known the subway to go so slowly.

On my way downtown I thought of my visit to Palestine in November, 1945. The publication of the Harrison report the preceding autumn had sent me off on my first visit to the Holy Land. I had wanted to see the country for myself. Like most American Jews I was neither a Zionist nor an anti-Zionist. The problem of "displaced" European Jewry — what a gingerly understatement that adjective embodies! — and the reported desire of the majority to go to Palestine had awakened my interest. I went out to estimate for myself the possibility of rebuilding their lives in that country. I fell in love with the place, with its vitality and its pioneering spirit. I understood the motivations behind the Return. Now it seemed to me, as I impatiently watched the subway stations go by, that perhaps I might have the opportunity of seeing something of the other side of the picture, of catching some glimpse of the migration itself and the conditions behind it.

When I met my friend at the railroad station, I asked him impatiently, "Where are we going?"

He was in a happy mood. "You'll see," he said, and led me by the arm to a train. He had the pleased look of a small boy with a surprise up his sleeve. But I had a bigger surprise for him. An idea had begun to form in my mind on the way down.

Late that night in a city near New York I met a group of two dozen American Jewish boys who were preparing to sail for Europe the next day. There they would be sent to a Mediterranean port where they would board one of the illegal ships and prepare to take it through the British blockade and into Palestine.

"Until now," my friend told me proudly, "we had depended on professional sailors attracted by good pay for a
dangerous mission. This ship will be the first to be manned
by American Jewish boys who volunteered their services
in a desire to help. Some are experienced sailors. Others
are going to sea for the first time.

I was flattered when some of the boys recognized me
and one said he had read my articles on Palestine in *PM*
and the *Nation*. There were drinks all around and then I
sprang *my* surprise.

"I'd like to go along," I told my Palestinian friend, "and
write the whole story of the voyage from the beginning
to the arrival in Palestine."

The boys were to sail the next day, and I said I was
prepared to come back in the morning and sail with them.
I said I was ready to board their illegal ship in Europe as
newspaperman, passenger, crew member or stowaway—
whichever was the most convenient. The proposal precipitated an argument.

Some liked the idea of having an official historian along
on the voyage, especially those who were *PM* fans. Others
feared that my presence might arouse suspicion in Europe.

It was finally agreed that I should be allowed to go
along, but my American friend warned me that there was
no point in my trying to sail next day with the boys. He
warned me that they would have to wait four to eight
weeks in Europe before an illegal ship and its passengers
were ready for them.

"I suggest," he said, "that you wait until an illegal ship
is ready to take on its cargo in Europe for Palestine.

You can then fly across to Europe in time to get on the boat before it embarks for the voyage across the Mediterranean."

We all agreed that that would be the wiser plan. But even this plan had to be somewhat tentative.

"We must tell you, however," my friend said, "that you cannot be absolutely certain of making the trip. Final decision will have to rest with *Haganah* officials in Europe. Circumstances might arise which would make it impossible for them to allow a newspaperman on one of the ships. You might fly across and then find that you could not embark after all."

I said I was willing to take the chance.

I was also warned that a great deal depended on my discretion. No other newspaperman had ever been permitted to travel the underground route to Palestine. "Any leak," I was told, "might be disastrous."

I told no one but my wife—the most discreet woman I know—and the two top editors of *PM* what I was planning to do. My chief on the *Nation*, Freda Kirchwey, was out of the country at the time, herself on the way to Palestine. I hoped my other colleagues on the *Nation* would forgive me for telling them that I was taking a leave of absence to cover the Paris Peace Conference for *PM*.

I applied for and obtained my passport, but getting a visa from the British for Palestine was a problem. I intended to go without a visa if the British refused to grant me one. At the British Embassy in Washington, the official in charge wanted to know what I intended to do as a newspaperman in Palestine. Was I, he inquired delicately, go-

ing to cover the—uh—Arabs or was I going to cover the
—uh—Jews? I pretended not to understand. I said it was
a small country and that to get a real story I'd have to
cover both.

The answer didn't satisfy him. He said I'd have to give
him $25 to cover the cost of a cable to the British infor-
mation officer in Jerusalem, presumably to ask whether I
was *persona grata*. The British don't like newspapermen
around their empire who fail to absorb the British point
of view. I remembered the troubles my friend, Constantine
Poulos, of Overseas News Agency had encountered in the
Middle East after he had sent a dispatch comparing British
actions in Palestine with their conduct in Greece, and I recalled also the difficulties which had piled up for the late
Ben Robertson of *PM* when he failed to see eye to eye with
the British on India. I told the Embassy visa officer that I
couldn't wait while he consulted the British authorities in
Jerusalem on my acceptability.

I went around to see a high official of the Embassy, a
gentle and scholarly Tory, who gave me my visa at once
after telling me pointedly that of course the British, unlike
the Russians, did not intend to hide behind an iron curtain. I thanked him. (When I got back I gathered that the
poor chap was in hot water with the Foreign Office for his
devotion to freedom of the press. Almost my first call on
my return to America was from my friend, Charlie Camp-
bell, the chief British information officer in Washington,
saying that London wanted to know how I had gotten my
visa.)

I spent an impatient month around Washington. The

day finally arrived when I got word that it was time to leave for Europe. It was the middle of May when I took off from La Guardia Field and headed for the North Atlantic.

III

I landed at Hurn airport the next day. From the train window on the two-and-a-half-hour ride to London, rural England had the appearance of a well kept garden. The cottages with their hedgerows, the green rolling downs, the dull yellow of the neat haycocks delighted the eye.

London was scarred and pitted. There were jagged edges in the skyline of chimney pots and palaces. Along the docks of the East End I saw whole blocks blasted and leveled. In the busy West End there was hardly a street that did not have some reminder of the blitz. Empty spaces gaped from among the buildings and weeds had begun to spring up in the rubble. There were buildings which seemed whole but turned out to be blind and hollow shells, their innards torn away.

In this dowager of imperial cities with its antique charm there was a reluctant admiration for, but also an undercurrent of resentment against America. American movies were everywhere, as were imitations of American advertising methods. But the contrast between Britain's continuing hardships and American prosperity was not made easier to bear by our own failure to meet food commitments to

Europe. America, to the meagerly fed Englishman, was a place where greedy folk ate ten meals a day.

I found these feelings reflected in the average Englishman's resentment over what he regarded as American interference in the Palestine problem. The British were sensitive about charges of imperialism, and in no mood to be preached to by America on imperial problems. No important country is as dependent as theirs on imports. To the ordinary Britisher at the moment the Empire meant the sterling bloc and the sterling bloc meant bread and butter.

The Englishman felt that his country was more generous than America in taking refugees during the Hitler period and the war. He regarded his standards of race tolerance as higher than our own. Palestine had been a British mandate, Zionism a British political issue, since the last war. There was great sentimental interest in the problem of a Jewish national home.

But at that moment, with a hundred and one (for him) far more urgent problems on his hands, the average Britisher was in no mood for risks in the Middle East. He had been sold the idea that further concessions to the Jews on Palestine would "inflame" the Arab world and he felt he had troubles enough without Arab uprisings.

In the noisy crowded bar of the House of Commons, one sensed that the Conservatives were resigned, the Laborites jubilant, over the current pledge to withdraw from Egypt. It was felt that the new White Paper on India was the answer to "nonsense" about the "continuity of foreign policy from the Tory to the Labor regime." But the plan to withdraw from Egypt seemed to have made the British

Government more intent than ever on keeping Palestine as a military base in the Middle East.

The Anglo-American Committee of Inquiry had just made its report on Palestine, unanimously recommending the admission of the 100,000 DP's from the German and Austrian camps and the ultimate establishment of a bi-national Arab-Jewish state in Palestine. I talked at the House of Commons one night with Richard H. S. Crossman, a Labor MP and one of the editors of the London *New Statesman and Nation.* Crossman's sympathy and courage as a member of the committee had been the principal factor in winning the British members to these unexpected unanimous recommendations. He was staking his political future in the Labor Party on the Palestine issue. I verified in London what Bartley J. Crum, the most militant American member of the committee, had charged in the United States—that Foreign Minister Ernest Bevin at a farewell luncheon to the committee in London had given his word that the British Government would put into effect any unanimous recommendations by the committee. It was already clear at the time I was in London that Bevin had no intention of keeping his promise.

I left London feeling that Jewish refugees could expect little sympathy from the average Englishman, and even less from the British Government. I was anxious to get on and see what the Jews could do for themselves, and took a boat train for the Continent.

IV

The city to which I was directed is one of the loveliest
on the Continent, but the people seemed hungry and cold.
There were no taxis, and I paid two hundred francs to an
extraordinarily thin but very intelligent porter who carried my bags to the hotel. I had been given instructions on
how to make contact with an underground *Haganah*
worker. The method was rather roundabout. My second
day I received word to be at a certain café at seven o'clock
that evening.

I was sitting outside the café at that hour, enjoying the
passing crowds, when a man tapped me on the shoulder
and asked me if I was I. F. Stone. I said I was and asked
him if his name was Jacques. My friend was the *schliach*
I had been told to contact.

The word *schliach* in Hebrew means "emissary." It is
applied to every sort of representative sent abroad by a
Palestinian Jewish organization, but is used more especially
for those men assigned by the *Haganah* for underground
rescue and illegal immigration work in Europe.

I will not do the British Intelligence Service the favor of
describing Jacques too closely. I came to know him well
during my stay abroad. He was a cultured person with a
sense of fun and adventure, but at the same time a man of
tremendous devotion to the task assigned him. If you can
imagine Galahad with a sense of humor you'll get a pretty

good spiritual picture of my friend—in fact those few people who know the underground workers in Europe will
recognize him at once from that description. I must say I
have never met a nobler group of human beings than the
Schlichim I encountered abroad.

In almost all Jewish organizations operating in Europe,
as in almost all social welfare groups, a certain unpleasant
and bureaucratic atmosphere is evident. An invisible
wall grows up between the people to be helped and those
doing the helping. I never felt any attitude of superiority,
condescension or patronage toward refugees among the
Haganah men working in the *Aliyah Beth.*

Many were men of wide education and experience. Some
had led lives of quiet scholarship before the war. Others
were members of farm collectives in Palestine. They had
stories to tell which cannot yet be published. Few people
have ever been fortunate enough to be served by men of
such ability and consecration to their task.

I was happy to learn from Jacques that I would be allowed to make the trip. I did not yet know how many difficulties still lay ahead of me.

"We have decided," the *Haganah* worker told me, "to
let you travel as a passenger on an *Aliyah Beth* boat and to
write about your experiences providing you use as few real
names as possible of people and places. The British are
making it harder for us every day to go on with our rescue
work."

I was disappointed to learn that I would not be able to
board a boat immediately.

"The *Aliyah Beth*," the *Haganah* worker told me with

a smile, "is far from being as well organized as a Cook's tour. The greatest exodus in the history of the Jewish people is under way in Europe. Refugees are seeping through every border in a desperate effort to get out of this hate-infested continent to Palestine. We're doing the best we can to help them, but that best is all too little. The one thing they cannot do unaided is to cross the Mediterranean, and that is where our major task comes in. But there are interminable difficulties and unforeseen delays. I don't know how soon I can get you on a ship."

The *Haganah* worker suggested that I spend a week acquiring visas for every country in the Mediterranean.

"The next ship may be leaving from France, or Italy, or Yugoslavia, or Greece, or Rumania. You'd better be prepared to fly to any one of those countries on a few hours' notice," he advised.

But after a week of visa gathering I still found myself with no sailing in prospect.

It was not easy to reach that *Haganah* worker. I had a telephone number but it was only that of a friendly businessman who in turn had to contact a third person who by roundabout ways forwarded messages to the *Haganah*. I was growing impatient and sought another meeting. When I finally managed to get in touch with the *Haganah* worker with whom I had first spoken, he suggested that I have a look at the DP camps in Germany and Austria, and then go on into Czechoslovakia, and, if there was still time, Poland.

"You might as well see for yourself," he said, "what conditions lie behind this migration."

I asked whether I might travel back from Poland via the underground. He warned against it.

"Conditions in Poland are very unsettled and Jews are often shot at by bandit or anti-Semitic gangs on their way out," he told me. "It would be better to come out by plane."

The *Haganah* worker gave me a list of underground contacts in Germany, Austria, Czechoslovakia and Poland, and he wrote out a kind of passport in Hebrew, saying that I was a newspaperman who could be trusted. I went to Paris and obtained temporary military orders for Germany from U. S. Army headquarters at the Hotel Majestic and filed an application at the Polish Embassy in Paris for a visa to Poland. Then I left on the Orient Express for Germany.

UNDERGROUND TO PALESTINE

I See the DP's

I See the DP's

I

Of Germany my first impressions were the rubble of the cities and the untouched rich green of the countryside. Crossing the Rhine on the train from Strasbourg into the French zone, I saw a wrecked bridge and then at Kehl, a ruined railroad station. On the platform lounged a few German prisoners in dirty dungarees and several French soldiers with red stripes down the side of their blue pants, like the toy soldiers we played with as children.

All along the line, at every station and in every town, the railroad stations were battered, houses gutted. But despite all I saw on the way, to walk out of the railroad sta-

tion in the lowering dusk of a rainy evening in Munic
was unexpectedly macabre. The railway plaza looked lik
a scene from the H. G. Wells movie *Things To Come*. Al
that was left of the few buildings which lined the plaz
were a few crazy brick skeletons, on one of which, high up
an undamaged bathtub protruded dizzily from a precariou
bit of wall. Through the broken windows I could see th
darkening sky. Piles of wreckage exuded the smell of un
buried bodies. The trams still ran, people moved abou
like ants in a ruined anthill, temporary booths at the sta
tion provided permits for the few taxis and also ratio
cards for Wurst-Butter-Käse (sausage, butter, and cheese)
but these evidences of life only made Munich seem all th
more like some dreadful nightmare.

Ninety miles north in medieval Nuremberg, where th
old walled city lay half ruined, the war crimes trial groun
on. I was there for a morning to see the impatience of th
dignified British chief justice, Lawrence, and to hear hir
say "Get on, get on," irritably, at the awkward cross-exam
nation and interminable leading questions of the clums
German defense lawyers. I heard Baldur von Schirach, th
Nazi youth leader, explain that he was one of the Jew
best friends. And as I watched that odd collection of shift
German burgers on trial, pasty faced and shabby, it seeme
to me that the ex-Supermen might have been a group o
middle aged, pompous German respectables caught in
raid on some shady establishment.

In the voluminous testimony through which I leafe
with *PM's* Victor Bernstein, I was struck by one vivid pas
sage. It was in the testimony of Rudolph Hess, the forme

ommandant of Auschwitz. Of the gas chambers he said,
We knew when the people were dead because they
topped screaming." Of the panic on the way to the cham-
ers: "Very frequently women would hide their children
nder their clothes, but of course when we found them we
vould send the children in to be exterminated."

II

Into this Germany of destruction, death, and dreadful
memories, Jews were pouring from Eastern Europe to wait
n opportunity to get to Palestine. It was ironical and dangerous that Germany should be the one country in Europe
n which the Jewish population was growing constantly,
nd serious trouble was possible there. The hatred of the
Iews for the Germans—in each of whom they saw the
murderer of parents, wives, and children—was not difficult
o imagine, though the most objective and dispassionate
view of the German problem I heard in the Reich was
from a seventeen-year-old Lithuanian Jewish boy I met on
a truck going to Landsberg. He did not regard the Germans as a lost people but as one badly poisoned. He thought
that given a long and wisely handled occupation they could
be rehabilitated and fitted into the framework of a decent
and progressive Europe. But I did not get this calm view
from most of the DP's with whom I talked.

The Germans themselves, obsequious or sullen, gav
me little sense of change and the few German progressive
with whom I talked, though they voiced optimistic view
betrayed their fear that they would be back in jail or con
centration camp again if and when the occupying power
left.

In Nuremberg I saw Social Democratic wall poster
pleading *"Deutsche Mütter! Willst du jemals weider dein
Söhne dem Krieg opfern?* ("German mothers! Do yo
wish ever again to sacrifice your sons to war?") But on
wondered whether some would not answer "yes" instead o
the "nein" with which the placard urged them to vote th
Social Democratic ticket. In tiny Amberg I heard a com
munist leader admit that Nazism had eaten "tief, sehr tief"
("deep, very deep") into the German working class an
that only a long occupation could re-educate these people
In the meantime it was easier for the Germans to fall bacl
on the old scapegoat: "The Jews are the cause of our mis
fortune," those fierce creatures streaming in from the Eas
who were not afraid to beat up the German policemen who
ventured into their camps. The American zone of Ger
many, with its hundred thousand restless Jews, still home
less and still far from free a year and a half after the liber
ation, seemed a human volcano in which bloody battle
might break out at any time and spread from town to town

Here a whole group of agencies were trying to do thei
best with a difficult and growing problem. The United
States Army, UNRRA, and the Joint Distribution Com
mittee had the job of providing homes, food, and clothing
Some of the camps, especially the transient centers, were

dreadful and dirty places. I visited one such center, run by UNRRA in a bombed-out Luftwaffe Signal Corps factory in Funk Caserne outside Munich. This was a reception and repatriation camp which had handled people of fifty-five different nationalities on their way home, including folk from as far as Ethiopia, Afghanistan, and Saudi Arabia. The stream of other nationalities was tapering off, but fifteen hundred Jews a month were still coming through there.

The harassed UNRRA staff did its best; I saw two truckloads of children, including small girls in braids, go off from the camp to a puppet show while I was there. Gardens had been planted and I was proudly shown the spotless white tile hospital built by the DP's themselves. But sleeping quarters for the transients were still in a huge and stinking third floor loft with three tiers of bunks. The center had room for twenty-three hundred transients, who were moved out to permanent camps as rapidly as possible.

"If conditions here were too good," one of my UNRRA guides said, "they'd stay on. This is only supposed to be a clearance center."

Jewish life in Germany was strange and full of contrasts. Not a half hour's drive from these filthy barracks which housed transient Jews at Funk Caserne, I visited the American Military Government headquarters in Munich. I was in the office of a former German Jewish refugee who had escaped before the war, gone to America, enlisted in the United States Army after Pearl Harbor, become a captain and been assigned to military government in his native land. He was a big fellow; his anteroom was full of admir-

ing German fraülein assistants and secretaries whom he
seemed to keep in a constant flutter. He appeared half
American, half Prussian. He was enjoying himself tremendously and his reverberating "*Jawohls*" on the telephone sounded like those of an old-fashioned Junker officer, tremendously pleased with himself and his authority

III

Conditions in the permanent camps varied considerably
The prize exhibit of the lot was the famous *kibbutz* on the
farm once owned by the notorious Nazi anti-Semitic pub-
lisher, Streicher, near Nuremberg. There, amid the green
rolling Franconian hills, DP's lived much the same life
they would live in Palestine. I saw them bring the cows
home at evening. I talked with their chief agronomist
Josef Heler, a Polish Jewish farmer from Galicia on the
Russian side of the Ribbentrop-Molotov line, who was sent
to a labor camp in Siberia as a *kulak* and freed after the
Stalin-Sikorski agreement. He became assistant director of
a ten-thousand-hectare beet-sugar farm near Djamboul in
Kazakstan. His wife and two children were killed by the
Germans during the invasion. The Russians wanted him
to stay in Kazakstan, but gave him his papers as a Polish
citizen repatriate when he insisted on leaving.

"I was well treated and had useful work in Kazakstan,"
Heler said, "but I left because having suffered as a Jew I

wanted to live as a Jew. I'm going to Palestine where I think my experience with similar agricultural conditions in arid Kazakstan will be very useful."

The communal kitchen, the simple dinner of sour cream, bread and butter, fresh vegetables, and coffee, the singing of the *Chalutzim,* reminded me of the colonies I had visited in Palestine in 1945. Heler told me that they not only raised all their own food but supplied milk to nearby DP camps.

"What about meat?" I asked him.

"Come, I'll show you," he said with an amused gleam in his eye.

He took me to the huge barns where he proudly showed me two of the biggest sows I have ever seen.

"Not exactly *kosher,*" he said, "but very tasty."

The largest camp I visited, one of the largest in Germany, was at the little Bavarian town of Landsberg in whose medieval fortress Hitler was imprisoned after the 1923 Munich beer-hall putsch. Here one saw a typical group of DP's—"die zweite categorie der Menschen" ("the second class of mankind") as one of the DP's there wryly described them to me. The camp was a collection of brick buildings in a kind of compound which had once been used as an artillery plant. What I first saw there was a lot of ill-dressed Jews walking about in a rather dispirited and desultory way in the courtyard. They were an unattractive lot. I walked through them to the main building—which has been renamed Roosevelt House—where I found the telephone operator in her cubbyhole at the entrance reading Henrietta Buckmaster's story of the slave South, *Deep*

River. The operator was a Polish Jewish girl, a DP, who read English better than she spoke it. In the building was a library, offices of various agencies and committees, and meeting rooms. The operator put me in touch with an UNRRA official who took me around.

The people in this camp seemed to fall into three groups. One was made up of pretty bad elements, people who had been hurt morally by the things they had to do to survive. Among them were black marketeers and petty speculators. They were a minority. A second group was made up of those who had little stamina left. They were living out of their suitcases as it were, anxious to go as soon as they could. In the meantime it was hard to get them to do much of anything. A third group was of people who were just as anxious to leave as the others but prepared to spend their time usefully while they waited. Among them were people of natural leadership and ability who organized schools and workshops and helped to train their fellows for a useful life elsewhere. Almost all of them wanted to go to Palestine.

Getting things done at Landsberg was often a challenge to ingenuity. The camp officials and the more enterprising DP's wanted to build a brick wall at the entrance.

"We couldn't get any bricks," one official told me, "so we had to tear down a brick air-raid shelter. To use these old bricks, we had to have special tools. We couldn't buy tools so we had to make them in our own workshop. But to make tools of raw metal, we had to have coke. To get the coke we pulled a deal with German officials in the town, swapped some things they wanted for the coke we needed."

I visited the schools at Landsberg and talked with the DP's who had helped to organize them. One of them was a young Polish engineer named Wolf Michelski. He was twenty-eight, slight of build and dark haired. He was from Kovno in Lithuania. He had been a construction engineer in his home town. His mother, sister, and father went to their deaths when the Germans liquidated the Kovno ghetto in 1944, but he was sent to a work camp in Stutthoff and later to Landsberg. There he worked in the artillery factory that now houses the DP's.

"Eighteen hundred able bodied Jews from the Kovno ghetto were sent to the German work camps," Michelski said, "but only four hundred survived.

"After the liberation we took equipment from the factory and began to organize a trade school. We repaired the old smithy, and now use it for metal work."

Michelski proudly showed me the smithy and the workshops adjoining it. The prize equipment was a mechanical saw and an electric planing machine. They had a carpenter's shop, a welding department and a radio school in which the students did all kinds of repair work for the camp.

"We teach fourteen different trades here," Michelski told me. "We have budding locksmiths, carpenters, shoemakers, tailors, dental technicians, photographers, radio repair men, electricians, auto mechanics, chauffeurs, farmers, and male nurses, and we hope soon to inaugurate a course for aviation mechanics."

Another of the leading personalities among the DP's in Landsberg was a young Polish Jew of thirty, Joe Buda, who

spoke good "American" English and from contact with
American soldiers had acquired the look and ways of a
typical GI. He was energetic, sandy haired, of medium
height. Joe was from Lodz, where his father owned a textile factory. He had an engineering degree from a Belgian
technical school where he studied from 1934 to 1938. He
had returned to Lodz to work as technical and engineering
director of his father's factory until the Germans came and
ordered all the Lodz Jews into a ghetto.

"I was betrothed," Joe told me, "and when the Germans
established the ghetto in Lodz my fiancée and I ran away
to Warsaw where we were married. The Germans put us
into a work camp. We ran away. For a time we hid in the
ghetto, and for a while we found work of a sort in the railway station at Warsaw. In 1942 the Germans caught me
and my wife again and sent us to Maidenek. We were separated. My wife was put in Field No. 4; I was put in Field
No. 5. We did no more than catch glimpses of each other
in the six months we were there. The last I saw of my wife
was when I managed to throw a kiss to her as I was being
taken away with other able-bodied men to a new work
place. She tried hard not to cry and so did I. I later heard
that she was sent to the gas chambers. None of my family
is left."

Joe and the man who taught dental technique at the
Landsberg camp took me on a memorable visit to a former
concentration camp nearby. The dentist's name was Dr.
Abel Akabas; he was a sturdy, dignified looking man from
Kovno, Lithuania. He had been an inmate of this concen-
tration camp, known as Lager No. 2, and he was one of the

ew who had survived. He survived because he was a dentist. It was his job to pull the gold teeth from the mouths of the dead, "sometimes," he told me grimly, "from heads without bodies." The gold was collected by the Nazis at the camp.

The camp was hidden away in a lovely emerald green forest off the main road to Landsberg. It was about a hundred yards square, surrounded by barbed wire. Inside were the bunkers in which the Jews lived. These were a kind of dugout, as long as a house and several feet underground, with peaked wooden roofs over them on which earth had been piled for warmth and on which grass grew.

Dr. Akabas took me to the dugout bunker in which he lived. Across the entrance was the derisive name "Sommerfreude" ("summer joy"). One had to stoop to enter. It was about five hundred feet square.

"About three hundred men lived in here, if you can call it living," Dr. Akabas told me; "about twenty-five died every day."

Our audience in the bunker was made up of four cows who looked at us with gentle, melancholy eyes. The concentration camp was already in use. A German woman lived in what had been the commander's house and stabled her cows in these bunkers where men had lived and died. She was a short, dumpy, irascible woman whose only reaction to our visit was to walk up angrily after we had left and slam the wire covered door behind us. We had forgotten to shut it firmly.

IV

It was a visit to a DP camp at Furth near Nuremberg
that helped me to understand vividly just how difficult i
was to live in these camps in Germany. The camp I visited
was run by a Major Cummings who worked for UNRRA
He was a stocky but dapper little Australian. He had fough
in the Australian Army in the First World War, worked
for the Anglo-Iranian Oil Company between the two wars
and served in the British Middle East command during the
Second World War. To judge only by that brief record
one might expect a rather unsympathetic person, with the
anti-Jewish prejudices some Britishers get in the Middle
East. But Major Cummings was one of the finest human
beings I met during my entire trip, a competent executive
and at the same time an extraordinarily kind and under
standing man.

You could judge the morale of a DP camp at once by
its cleanliness or lack of it. This camp outside Furth was
clean. There were curtains and flowerpots in the windows
of the houses in the camp, a sure sign of good morale.
Many of the people were orthodox Jews from Carpatho-
Russia in what was Eastern Czechoslovakia and is now
part of the Soviet Union. They had a synagogue and were
building themselves a theater. Outside the commissary
and the bakery, which smelled of fresh bread, was a notice
in Yiddish and English explaining the rationing system

n the camp and the amounts of food available per person.

"We try to explain everything to the people here," Major Cummings told me. "Things work out better if hey know exactly what's going on."

He showed me the gardens in which the DP's raised heir own vegetables. At one point I began talking to a group of refugees and asked what they would do about he German problem. It was a bad question. They got pretty excited. Afterward at lunch Major Cummings said: "You know they're a very emotional people." The average Englishman, brought up in the tradition of emotional restraint, would have said it in a tone of superiority, probably with contempt. Major Cummings said it in a fatherly way, as one who did not wish me to get a bad impression of the people in his charge.

I went around the camp by myself, looking into the various apartments and talking with people. They were clean and in good condition. In one apartment I talked with a Polish Jew, a former textile worker from Lodz, which was a center of the Polish textile industry. Unlike so many of the Polish Jews he was not undersized but a healthy and vigorous looking man. He told me he had lost his family and he praised the camp and its director.

"It's one of the best camps in Germany," he said, "and we couldn't have a more understanding director. But it's still no home."

He added a sentence that hit me hard.

"When I look out my window," he confided, "and see the barbed wire, *es wert mir kalt in herzen* (my heart grows cold) and when I go with my *tepele* (my little pot) to get my meals, I feel as though I'm still in *katzet* (concentration camp)."

V

I think I learned most about Germany when I got lost on my way from Nuremberg to Czechoslovakia and went to Amberg instead of Bamberg. I didn't know a soul in the town and the signs pointing to PRO, which I took joyfully to mean the Press Relations Officer, led only to a prophylactic station. I was traveling on Army orders and in military correspondent's uniform, so I was given a billet at the little officers' club. I set out to explore the town. It is what one would have described sentimentally two decades ago as a Hans Christian Andersen kind of town until we all learned what horrors can come out of these quaint little places with their ancient churches, arched bridges, and the stork nests on their chimneys.

It was evening and I walked down the main street to the town hall which is now the American Military Government headquarters. Nearby, as though for safety, were a Social Democratic party headquarters which was closed and a Communist party headquarters which was open. I went in to have a look at the pamphlets on display in the window and bought a set of them. One was an illustrated pamphlet on Buchenwald and its horrors. Another was on the war guilt of the German Reich and the *Mitschuld* of the German people (*mitschuld* is, literally, *with guilt,* that is, the fact that the people shared the guilt of the government).

There were three men in the combination party headquarters and bookshop. One of them seemed to be the communist leader of the town. I began to understand how many communists managed to survive under Hitler. They survived by abstaining from political activity. One of the men, an engineer, had been in jail four months as a political prisoner at the beginning of the Hitler period and afterwards was kept under surveillance. He had to report to the police regularly and was permitted only manual labor jobs. He was warned not to try to work in any arms plants, and he told me frankly that he had been able to do no political work. The one who seemed to be the leader spent a year and two months in Dachau for giving out anti-Nazi leaflets, and also lived by avoiding any political activity afterwards.

He told me that Amberg and its vicinity was rightist territory. Forty per cent of the people could not vote because they had been Nazis, and two-thirds of the remainder had voted the right wing Christian Socialist party ticket at the local elections. Thirty per cent voted Social Democratic and one per cent Communist. He complained that the AMG officers were partial to this right wing party but admitted that if the Americans left, the Germans would probably have the communists and socialists in jail again in a year or so. He felt that only a long occupation could change the character of the people.

I asked him whether he thought Jews could now live in Germany.

"Es ist sehr schlecht" ("it's very bad"), he answered.

He didn't think there was much hope of re-establishing Jews in Germany for a long time. I asked how many Jews were left in that town and he told me only forty. One of the communists offered to take me to their synagogue.

When I got there I found not local Jews but Polish Jewish refugees. They lived together in the community center and most of them were in the courtyard when I entered. The synagogue had been newly rebuilt thanks to help from the American Army, and its sacred utensils had been returned by a German who took them and hid them when the synagogue was burned in 1938. Upstairs they had a common mess hall, sleeping quarters and a library with a very old collection of books in English, Yiddish, and Hebrew, including *The Education of Henry Adams* and several dialogues of Plato. In the office of this center there were two pictures. One, a small one, was a picture of Theodore Herzl, the Viennese journalist who founded the Zionist movement. The other, a very large picture, was a picture of their hero and messiah, Sergeant M. Rubinoff of Portland, Maine. Sergeant Rubinoff, who had a round, good-natured Jewish boy's face, was the first American Jewish soldier to get into the town. He found seventy-five Jews in an UNRRA tuberculosis sanatorium, got them food and clothing and helped rebuild the synagogue. He still sent them letters and packages from Portland.

Two of the Polish Jews took me to visit the last remaining German Jew in Amberg and its surrounding territory.

We went up a narrow alley into a medieval house with earthen floor, up three rickety flights of stairs to an apartment in which we found a seventy-six year old Jewish woman, Clara Lorsch, having a bit of gingerbread with a middle aged German woman who was one of her neighbors. She was born, she told me in a creaking voice, in Steinach an der Saale, but had lived forty years in Amberg where she had a small shop. She was a widow. She remembered with gratitude that when the local Nazi commissar closed her shop up and confiscated its goods in 1938, he first granted her request to be allowed to take out linens for her own use and that of her daughter-in-law, who was now dead. She also remembered that even after 1938 her neighbors had greeted her in the streets when they saw her. Once a peasant woman gave her food. In 1941 she was sent to Theresienstadt and spent three years in a concentration camp. The old lady had a wry sense of humor.

"I have become the miracle of Amberg," she said, referring to the interest in her as the only native German Jew in that area.

She was leaving to spend her last years with her son, Dr. K. F. Lorsch, a London physician, whom she had not seen for many years.

Her neighbor, whom she had called in to share the gingerbread she had made, was very ingratiating and obsequious to us. But every once in a while this thin, spinsterish German woman would steal a glance at the two dark Polish Jews with me, a look of fascinated horror as though she expected rape at any moment, as in the passage in *Mein Kampf* about the dark Jew lying in wait for the blond Aryan maiden.

My last memory of Amberg and of Germany was the chat I had with the bartender in the officers' club that night. He showed me his Wehrmacht (German army papers). He was a nice person and he pleaded that the German people must have "work and bread." But at the end of our talk he shook his head sadly and said in German:

"If he (meaning Hitler) came again and screamed, they'd follow him like sheep once more."

UNDERGROUND TO PALESTINE

Underground Railway To Bratislava

Underground Railway to Bratislava

I

I had been visiting frontier posts and had reached the railroad station just in time. I ducked under the gates at the crossing, ran across the tracks, and jumped on the rear car. It was 4:25 on a June afternoon in a little Czech town near the Polish border. I will call it Anton.

I had arrived there only that morning. From sleepy Amberg in Germany I had made my way to Schwandorf and Furth-i-Wald, thence over the Czech border to Pilsen and Prague. In gloomy, medieval Prague the Polish Embassy had no word from Warsaw on my application for a visa. I decided to make my way to the Polish-Czech border,

41

in the hope of joining a group of refugees on the border and traveling with them on the underground route to Palestine.

I had been lucky. I found myself at one of the most popular crossing points on the Polish-Czech frontier on the very day a transport was about to leave for Bratislava. In that Slovak capital a hundred and eighty miles to the southeast, they hoped to cross the Austrian frontier illegally into the Russian zone and proceed from there to Vienna.

I wore the military correspondent's uniform which I had acquired in the American military zone in Germany. The Czechs lounging on the station platform looked surprised to see an American in uniform swinging aboard that last car. Its grimy windows and decrepit appearance set it off unmistakably from the rest of the train.

I was traveling light and had only a briefcase and a brown canvas zipper bag. I heard someone on the last car shout in Yiddish: "Look, the American is coming with us!" Friendly hands grabbed my bags and helped me up into that ancient wooden third-class carriage. It was about one-third the size of an American railroad car and it was packed with Jewish refugees. They had seen me earlier in the day at the Czech Red Cross hospital through which they clear. They recognized me and I was greeted with *sholoms* (literally, in Hebrew, *peace*—the equivalent of our *hello*).

The car we were in had the European style side aisle, compartments with long wooden seats and one small washroom with a tap from which no water ran. The car was dirty and crowded. Later, when I counted my fellow passengers, I found there were fifty-five of us. All but two were Jewish refugees who had managed to make their way across the border from Poland into Czechoslovakia; among them were fourteen women and four small children, the youngest three, the oldest ten. A Czech and I were the other two.

The Czech, a thin friendly man in his fifties, told me he was a member of the secret police. He had been assigned by the Czech Government to see us to our next destination, Bratislava, the capital of Slovakia, about one hundred and eighty miles to the southwest. His job was to see that none of us got off the train before then, and, I suppose, to keep order if necessary. He was half guard, half escort. He told me, in a talk we had during the night, that he served in the Czech Legion during the First World War.

I had hardly caught my breath in the aisle before I was approached by fellow passengers. They examined the correspondent's patch on my shoulder and at once wanted to know if the *Herr Korrespondent* knew their uncle in "Jigago" or their cousin so-and-so in "Nefyork." Would I take their names and the names of their relatives in America for my paper? I promised I would.

As soon as the train began to move, everybody began to sing. The first song whose words I could make out was a Yiddish song written by a young man I was to meet soon. It was called *Chalutzim, Greten Sich Fahr Eretz Israel* (Pioneers Prepare Themselves for Palestine). The singing was spontaneous and joyful.

I was aware of the trials which lay ahead. I had seen
some of the thousands waiting in the DP camps of Austria
and Germany. I knew of the endless and exasperating
diplomatic negotiations between America and Britain over
the admission of one hundred thousand to Palestine. I had
heard of the dangers and delays which beset the underground route to Palestine, but there was no apprehension
among my fellow voyagers. They felt themselves on their
way.

Behind were the green hills of the treacherous Polish-
Czech border. Ahead somewhere were security, freedom,
and a new home. Their determination and confidence in-
fected me. It is only in retrospect that I feel the anxieties
we should have felt that day as we started off from Anton.

I was rescued from the importunate address bearers by
two young *Chalutzim* who wanted me to sit with them.
They picked up my bags and made a seat for me in one
of the compartments. There were ten *Chalutzim* in it,
youngsters in their teens and early twenties, and an older
man in his thirties, a Polish Jew with a mandolin.

Chalutzim means *pioneers* in Hebrew and is the term
for people who have been in training for life in a setle-
ment in Palestine. They are the Zionist élite, dedicated to
the building of Palestine. The ten I was with, five boys
and five girls, had all trained for several months in the
same *kibbutz* (collective training settlement) in Poland.
It was a *kibbutz* near Lodz called *Dror* (Freedom), sup-
ported by funds of the Poale Zion, the Labor Zionist
movement.

As our train rattled along over the Czech countryside,

past green farms and tiny villages, the *Chalutzim* told me of the trouble they had had getting across the border. Their experience was an unusual one. They were the only group I encountered in all my travels whose difficulties had occurred on the Czech rather than the Polish side of the border. A friendly Pole led them across the Polish frontier. Unfortunately they reached the Czech side not at the hospitable town of Anton, but about twenty-five miles away in a small Czech city where the police ordered them back to Poland.

The *Chalutzim* told the police: "You can shoot us but you can't force us to go back into Poland." They were a ragged but determined lot of youngsters, and the Czech police must have realized that they meant it. The guards let them in and put them on a train for the clearance center at Anton, but they had to change trains halfway there, and at the halfway point the conductor wouldn't let them on the next train because they had no tickets and no money. The police at the station again ordered them back to Poland, and again they challenged the police: "You can shoot us, but we're not going back." The police finally put them on another train and told the conductor to let them ride free to Anton. There they found their way to the Red Cross hospital.

Twenty-five miles away from Anton, our train stopped at a local station and I could see that we were in for a long, slow ride. The locomotive was a museum piece that looked as if it would burst its boilers if it went faster than twenty miles an hour. I got out with some of the others to stretch my legs on the platform and began talking to the man with the mandolin.

The man with the mandolin was not a *Chalutz*. He was a leather worker from Sosnowice in Poland. He had been a *Mizrachi* (conservative, religious) Zionist before the war and was on his way to Palestine. He told me his story, and he told it in the matter-of-fact way all the refugees I met spoke of their personal tragedies. For them, the hurt was too deep and familiar for tears.

"There were twenty-five hundred Jews in Sosnowice before the war," he said. "There are very few left now. Shortly after the Germans came, they sent us all into a ghetto. There my wife and I worked for the Gestapo as tailors. We had a six-year-old daughter.

"In 1943 the Germans liquidated the ghetto. All but three thousand able-bodied workers were sent away, as we discovered later, to be burned in the crematoriums. My wife and child were among them. I went with the workers to Auschwitz and later to Buchenwald."

He showed me the tattooed concentration camp number on his arm, 134571. I saw few Jewish arms in Europe without a tattooed number. The Jews show it to you proudly as a badge of honor.

"When my wife and child were sent away," the man continued, "my wife cried out to me: '*Mein theurer* (my dear), when the war is over come look for us.' After those of us who survived were liberated from Buchenwald, I went back to Poland to see if I could find any trace of my wife and child. All I located was a sister-in-law who told me she had seen them on their way to the death furnaces."

When we were back in the train and had started off again, I asked him where he got the mandolin. He said that when the Germans sent him to the ghetto, he gave the mandolin for safekeeping to the Polish janitor of the apartment house in which he and his wife had lived. When he got back to Sosnowice he looked up the janitor, recovered his mandolin and started off on the road to Palestine.

"This," he said in Yiddish, "is all that remains of my old life."

So he played and the *Chalutzim* sang.

II

Before boarding the train, my comrades had succeeded in getting over one of the most dangerous frontiers in Eastern Europe.

By day this Polish frontier was deceptively peaceful—rolling grassy farmlands, gently rising mountains, cool forests and quiet villages with wayside shrines.

I had walked there among the same wild flowers we know back home: daisies, buttercups, dandelions, red clover and white, and Queen Anne's lace. Bees hummed in the apple orchards and at one point a brook sang in the no-man's land between the Czech and Polish frontier posts.

Seeing this border on a sleepy summer afternoon, it was hard to believe that at night this restful countryside was the setting for a nightmarish game of hide-and-seek between refugees and Polish frontier guards.

I had seen some of these guards and a bit of their handiwork on my visit to the border. In one Czech frontier village, the Czech and Polish border posts are less than one hundred feet apart. Between them was a white stucco farmhouse, with an elaborately carved wooden birdhouse perched high up beside it. There was a busy coming and going in the birdhouse, but the farmhouse stood deserted.

In the village I met the Czech who used to live in that house. He had a patch over his left eye and lifted the patch to show me an empty socket. The eye had been shot out by Polish border guards, who accused him of being a Czech spy. Since the shooting, he had moved out of his old home in that miniature but dangerous no-man's land and into the security of the village.

The Czech told me that he had lived in Breslau, then German Silesia, before the war. He had been an active anti-Fascist, had served a term in the prison at Breslau during the Hitler period, and been sent by the Nazis to Buchenwald for underground activity.

"You see that farmhouse up there," he said in German, pointing further up the frontier. "A Czech woman who lived there was murdered one night a few months ago. No one knows who killed her, but we all suspect it was done by Polish frontier guards."

I had bought a round of drinks for the Czech gendarmes in the village at a low-roofed tavern. They took me up to the border but would not let me approach the frontier gate until they had first spoken with the Polish guards on the other side and handed out some American cigarettes I had given them. I don't know why they took all these precautions. I hardly thought they would shoot a man in American uniform in broad daylight, no matter how close I came to the border. But the Czech gendarmes wouldn't let me walk up until they had established friendly contact.

The two Polish guards had walked across no-man's land to get the cigarettes. They shook hands with me across the barrier. In their makeshift uniforms, with knee patches on their trousers and ill-matched jackets, they looked like a pair of fierce *sans culottes* out of the French Revolution. Both had rifles slung over their shoulders. Conversation was limited, and my Czech friends and I soon went back to the tavern for another round of the local cherry brandy.

From the Czech gendarmes that afternoon and from my comrades on the train late that night, I heard a good deal about the difficulties and dangers encountered by illegal emigrants on the Polish side of the frontier.

On the border, Jews attempting to leave Poland run a double hazard. The first lies in the widespread anti-Semitism which affects both the Polish peasantry along the border and the border guards. The other lies in the general lawlessness existing in the country: armed bandits and underground Polish oppositionists who are both anti-Semitic and opposed to the present government.

To get by the frontier posts and the border patrols unseen is not easy, but a few refugees manage it, sometimes after many nights of watchful waiting in deep forest and high-grassed meadow. One man on the train told me he had come across the border with five other men and two children. He said it took them five weeks of waiting before they could find a way across without being seen by the Polish guards.

Most refugees are caught on their way over. Occasionally they may find a Polish frontier guard who will let them pass. More often they are stripped of all valuables and any clothing of value before being allowed to proceed to the more hospitable Czech side. Some remain on the border in unmarked graves. There are few nights without some shootings on the frontier.

The crossing is difficult enough for the men. It is a fearful experience for the women and children. Some are beaten by guards on the way over. There were several bandaged heads on the train.

Sometimes a group of refugees finds a hidden route across, or a frontier guard susceptible to bribery. One or two of the braver may return to Poland to help other groups over the frontier. A famous woman leader of the Warsaw ghetto uprising made the return trip four or five times in the region I visited, coming back each time with another group of refugees until her activities became too conspicuous, and she was forced to go on. She is now living in Palestine.

From what the refugees told me it was apparent that there were both a push and a pull across the border. The push was out of Poland. The pull was toward Palestine.

There was a sturdy, broad-shouldered, jolly little Polish

Jew on the train, about five feet four. He was the only other man except myself in the crowd with a complete costume. Somehow, in the distribution of cast-off clothing from America to refugees on the Czech side, he had fallen heir to a green chauffeur's uniform in good condition. Its neat lines and high collar gave him a military appearance he had earned. For he had fought two years as a soldier in the Red Army and then three years in the Polish Army. He was a Polish Jew who was lucky enough to get across the Russian border early in the war. He returned to his native land as a soldier in the Polish Army and helped to liberate Warsaw.

"And do you know the reception I got?" he asked me in Yiddish. "I meet a Polish woman and she says to me . . . I, who am a soldier in Polish uniform, mind you, and she knew I was a Jew . . . to *me,* she said, 'The one bad thing about Hitler is that he didn't kill all the Jews.' Do you think I wanted to stay in Poland after that?"

My stalwart little friend's story was substantially the same story I heard over and over again on the trip: Jews returned from concentration camps in Germany or from service in Russia; they very rarely located a relative or friend alive; they found whole Jewish communities destroyed; and they felt themselves unwelcome, despised, and hated in an atmosphere of virulent anti-Semitism.

"The Polish government is not anti-Semitic," I heard over and over again, "but the Polish people are. The government's hold is weak. Conditions are lawless. Life is dangerous. The government is trying its best to establish new colonies and homes for the Jews, but the task is hopeless. We have no future in Poland. We see only more pogroms ahead."

The "pull" toward Palestine I heard expressed again and again, not only from the young *Chalutzim* on the train, but from older folk who would say, "I'm not a Zionist. I'm a Jew. That's enough. We have wandered enough. We have worked and struggled too long on the lands of other peoples. We must build a land of our own. *Mir mussen bauen a Yiddish land.* (We must build a Jewish land.)"

There are few sights more depressing than one's first look at these Jews fleeing across the border. I had seen them earlier in the day in the Czech Red Cross hospital to which they are taken for a medical examination and clearance. The building had been a Hitler Youth hostel during the occupation. The smell from the basement latrines as we entered was overpowering. I got used to bad smells on the trip but I never encountered anything to match that first whiff in the hospital at Anton.

Through that thick and stinking atmosphere one came into a kitchen in which refugee women were preparing a one-dish meal of soup in two huge cauldrons. Beyond the kitchen was a dining room full of newly arrived refugees and a big room in which they were passing through their first medical examination.

They looked and smelled bad. Most of the men were undersized and underfed. The women were either scrawny or unhealthily obese, broad-beamed, and squat. The eyes of the children were the eyes of little people unpleasantly adult before their time. Men, women, and children, crowded together in that first reception center, ragged and unclean and tired, looked like the cast-offs of humanity.

The big news about the Jews of Eastern Europe is not that they have suffered. That is an old story, grown weary in the retelling. The real news is that so many of these people came across the border with tremendous vitality, with spirits unbroken.

Everywhere else in Europe I felt a defeatist spirit. In France again and again I heard it said *"France est fini"* ("France is finished"). In Vienna young Austrians told me, "We are tired. The old Vienna will never come again. There is no future for Austria." In Italy one found the same weariness and hopelessness.

These Jews out of the East who have suffered more than any other people in the war in terms of sheer numbers slain, who returned to find themselves without home or family, have a will to live and a will to build that are wonderful to see.

I made many friends and *chaverim* on the long journey. I came to love these people among whom I traveled. And I understood why they broke into song as our train began to move out of Anton on a journey many of them would wait months, or forever, to complete.

III

The refugees I was with were lucky to be starting their underground trip to Palestine from the little town of

Anton on the Polish-Czech border. The story of Anton
and its friendly attitude as I heard it on the train to Bratislava was, in large part, the story of two Czech Jews who
lived there. I will call them Schweik and Hacek. Those
were not their real names. These two, in their quiet, un-
dramatic and hard-working way, were heroes of the illegal
immigration. They had been willing to risk their high
standing in their community and their friendly relations
with their non-Jewish neighbors to help less fortunate
Jews across the border and on their way to Palestine.

There were three hundred Jews before the war in this
Czech town of twelve thousand. Only twenty survived.
Schweik and Hacek were the first of the survivors to come
home. Both came of old Czech-Jewish families. Schweik
was a captain in the Czech Legion in the first World War,
and became a successful manufacturer afterward. Hacek
was also a local businessman. Both were sent to Auschwitz
concentration camp by the Germans after the Czech occupation. One lost his parents and a brother; the other, his
wife, child, and four sisters to the concentration camp and
the crematorium.

Since their return, the government had restored not
only their property but that of their dead relatives, and
they had devoted their time and money to helping the
illegal immigration.

I first heard of Schweik and Hacek in Prague from an
underground worker to whom I had come along a kind
of chain of command, and I went to see them as soon as I
arrived in Anton. I located Schweik's office not far from
the railroad station. The office was an oak-paneled affair

that would have done credit to an up-and-coming business-man in America. I showed underground credentials I carried in Hebrew. I told him I had heard of the work he and his friend were doing, that I would like to see something of it and then join the next illegal transport leaving the town of Anton.

Schweik phoned Hacek to join us at lunch in Schweik's home. Both were tall, fine-looking men, and both had concentration camp numbers tattooed on their arms.

Lunch in Schweik's old-fashioned three-story brick home was served by an elderly Czech woman who had worked for the family many years before the war. Schweik assured me she spoke better Yiddish than he did. I found that easy to believe since the Yiddish of the Czech Jews is more German and Czech than Yiddish. This is the story Schweik told me:

The infiltration of refugee Jews into the town of Anton began during the revolution near the close of the war, when the Czechs rose against the German occupation authorities. There was a concentration camp for Jewish women in the neighborhood and about five hundred and sixty of these women were freed during the revolution and went to Anton. They lived in makeshift emergency lodgings for several weeks and then moved on into DP camps in Germany.

Schweik and Hacek, as the first native Jews to return to the town from concentration camp, did their best to furnish food and lodging to other concentration camp survivors who went through the town on their way back to their old homes.

"First," Schweik said, "people came through on their way back to Poland, but pretty soon a movement began in the opposite direction. Polish Jews began to return from Poland. They would tap on the windows in the middle of the night and ask for shelter. During the winter some came to us barefoot in the snow. The stories they told were much alike. They could find no trace of their families. The Polish government was not anti-Semitic, but the Polish people were. They preferred to return to the camps in Germany and wait for a chance to emigrate abroad to America or Palestine."

The work Schweik and Hacek did for these refugees had made them legendary figures among the Polish Jews. The "grapevine" had spread the fame of these two Czechs not only in Poland, but deep across the border into the Soviet Union. Sitting in that darkened dirty carriage, slowly making its way across the green Czechoslovakian countryside, I spoke with several Polish Jews from the USSR who had gone to Anton beccause of Schweik and Hacek.

"I first heard of them in Kazakstan," one Polish Jew told me. "I heard that the best place to cross the Polish-Czech border was at Anton, and that if one asked there for *Pan* Schweik or *Pan* Hacek one could be sure of a night's lodging and of help in making contact with the underground."

I gathered that at one time the popularity of Anton began to embarrass the local Czech authorities. About four months ago so many Jews had piled into the town that the authorities arrested some, but the result of that affair was only to further regularize the immigration.

Until that time Schweik and Hacek had carried the burden of the work unaided. This consisted, I gathered, not only in providing food, shelter, and transportation, but in facilitating passage over the border.

"I have good friends in America," Schweik said, with a smile, "who keep me plentifully supplied with American cigarettes. You can do a great deal in Europe today with a few cartons of American cigarettes."

Schweik and Hacek literally traded cigarettes for lives. They had friendly contacts with guards on both sides of the border, and a carton of cigarettes at the right spot often eased the way for a whole group of illegal emigrants.

At one time Schweik and Hacek appealed to UNRRA for aid and UNRRA sent an executive to the town, but he reported that there was no way under UNRRA regulations by which it could help. In December, 1945, the Joint Distribution Committee began to send Schweik and Hacek funds to cover the cost of food and tickets from Anton to Bratislava. And after the arrests the Czech Red Cross and the local authorities made a hospital available as a clearance and medical center for the "infiltrees."

Schweik and Hacek told me that five thousand Jews had come across the border through their town during the preceding twelve months. Between May 1 and June 4 alone there were 1,530 immigrants. The day before I got there, one hundred and forty-eight crossed the border and the day I was there fifty-one came over. They told me they expected a hundred or more the next day. I didn't ask how they knew this. One does not ask too many questions on the underground route.

Over the border in this area came Czechs and Germans as well as Jews, and some odd characters occasionally turned up. One time eight German SS men were discovered among the Jewish refugees. A Czech doctor supervising medical examinations saw the tattoo marks all SS men bear under their armpits, and turned them over to the Czech police.

There were two kinds of Jewish refugees coming across the Czech border. One was made up of Polish Jews who had returned from German concentration camps only to find life intolerable in their old homes. The other consisted of those Polish Jews who had fled into Russia after the war began or lived in the eastern territories annexed by the Soviet Union under the Ribbentrop-Molotov pact. Those who wished to return did so legally under the Russo-Polish repatriation agreement.

There was one striking difference between these Jews from Russia and those pouring into the underground from the European countries which were under Nazi domination or influence. Out of the Soviet Union alone came the miracle of whole Jewish families. Only among these refugees did one see fathers and mothers with children.

I heard of no Polish Jews coming out of Russia because they wanted to live in Poland. All those I talked with—and I encountered many on the underground route—left with the intention of making their way out of Poland. Most of them wanted to go to Palestine. Their favorite exit route seemed to be to take trains in Poland for the new areas of Jewish resettlement in the Silesian areas annexed by Poland and then to jump the train and head for the Czech border. This was not as easy as it sounds. Perhaps one in a hundred succeeded in getting across. There were some eighty thousand Jews waiting in the Silesian territory for a chance to get out of Poland.

Many of the Jews coming out of Russia had covered incredible distances. Jews from as far away as Vladivostok had crossed in the region I visited. One Polish Jewish physician with his whole family, including his seventy-five-year-old father, came through from Tibet; the physician had a brother who was president of the Joint Distribution Committee Fund in Venezuela. It took this physician and his family four months to reach Moscow from Tibet. Three days before my visit, one repatriated refugee from a small town four thousand meters east of Irkutsk crossed the border with ten children.

Western Czechoslovakia was a favorite crossing place for the illegal immigration. By western Czechoslovakia I mean Bohemia and Moravia, the Czech lands, for Czechoslovakia was a house divided between the democratic and cultured Czech country in the west, and backward peasant Slovakia in the east. Nowhere in eastern and central Europe were Jewish refugees more humanely treated than in the Czech provinces. But Slovakia, in this as in other respects, was a different story. Slovakia was an "independent" state under the Nazis and collaborated with them. It was a backward region culturally, under reactionary clerical influence, a festering place of Fascism and anti-Semitism. It was far easier for Jewish refugees to cross the Czech border, though they managed to get across the Slovak one, too.

The refugees I was traveling with all wondered what would be our own reception on Slovak soil. What would happen when we got to Bratislava, the capital of Slovakia?

"Do you think they'd dare to try and send us back," one youthful *Chalutz* asked me, "or will we be able to go on from there to Vienna?"

IV

We were not the only travelers of our kind in the wake of World War II. At way stations and on the sidings to which we were shunted to let more important trains pass, we saw other trains loaded with refugees. In ancient third-class carriages like ours we saw Poles going east, and in battered freight cars *Volksdeutsche* going west. It was easy to recognize freight cars carrying refugee cargo. They were almost always crudely decorated with branches and fresh green leaves.

The *Volksdeutsche* were a special kind of Germans, the creation of the Nazi regime. Among those we passed were Polish citizens of German ancestry, never too welcome in the old Poland, who had enjoyed a brief period as *Herren-volk* during the Nazi occupation. Officially they were being repatriated. Actually they were being expelled by the Po-land they had betrayed. They were bound for a Germany some of them had never seen. I had encountered some of

these *Volksdeutsche* in the Reich on my way to Czechoslovakia, and I knew that now that Germany had been defeated they were returning with resentment and anxiety.
There would be no joy of homecoming for them. I never
heard the *Volksdeutsche* sing.

I never heard singing from the Polish cars either. Some
of the returning Poles were ex-prisoners of war, but most
of them, like the Polish Jews with whom I was traveling,
had been in German concentration camps. They were
going home like the *Volksdeutsche,* in apprehension. The
DP camps from which they had come were largely under
the control of anti-Government Poles, drawn from the
Anders' Army. Even when these camp officials advised
their people to go home, the advice was hardly couched
in encouraging terms.

I heard of one Polish aristocrat who went back to Poland
secretly and illegally to see for himself before deciding
what to tell the displaced Poles under his care.

"Go back to Poland," he told his people when he returned. "Most of you were peasants, as were your fathers
before you. You knew nothing of politics before and you
know nothing of politics now. The land you tilled is still
there, and it must be tilled again, whatever the régime.
That is your place. Go back to it."

But he did not go back with them.

Sometimes our train and the trains carrying the other
refugees stopped on opposite sides of the same platform,
and people from both got out to stretch their legs. But
there was no mixing. No one shouted across the platform
from one train to the other. Their mutual misery created

no common bond between peoples who regarded each other as oppressors and oppressed. The hate and fear that flowed between us was almost tangible, like a thick current in the hot summer night.

"They have one advantage over us," an elderly Jew with a beard said to me in Yiddish, during one of these encounters. "They at least have a country of their own."

Our homelessness was reflected in the squeamish terminology applied to Jewish refugees. We were DP's—displaced persons. The term itself, for victims of Hitlerism, was a model of detached and frigid understatement. Some of us were Polish Jews repatriated from the Soviet Union, but others were Polish-Jewish DP's who were coming back from Poland—where the "displaced" had presumably been "replaced"—to the DP camps in the American zone of Germany and Austria.

For these people, official parlance had created a new category and a new euphemism: "Unsuccessful repatriatees." Even the shameful illegality of our border crossings had been covered with a custom-made, polysyllabic and refined little fig-leaf. We were "infiltrees." But nowhere in the records were my comrades referred to simply as Jews, although it was as Jews that they had suffered, and it was as Jews that most of them wanted a chance to live.

There wasn't too much food on the train. At the Red Cross hospital, on the Polish-Czech border, each of the refugees had been given a large loaf of dark rye bread for the trip to Bratislava. In their rucksacks and bags, buried in their few bits of clothing, many had hidden a jar of jam or a bit of sausage or cheese. A few had acquired, somewhere, somehow, small cans of sardines. A good many had a clove of garlic to rub on the bread and a bit of salt. Those men on the train who carried jack-knives passed them around to cut the bread, but many people just broke off pieces to eat. They ate heartily. On my underground trip I was to learn what a good meal could be made of dark brown bread with garlic rubbed over it, and salt.

I had a special treat for the comrades with whom I traveled. All they had to eat was bread, but I had come well prepared. I had gone shopping in Anton in preparation for the trip. I bought a kilo (two and two-tenths pounds) of sausage, a half dozen large white rolls, and a pound of assorted pastry. We had a grand meal together. The eyes of the *Chalutzim* lit up when they saw the sausage. The white rolls were as great a delicacy.

At first they politely declined both the sausage and the white rolls.

"That's your supper," they said. "We have plenty to eat."

But, after a little coaxing, they succumbed to the smell of the sausage, and pretty soon we had everything divided up evenly as befits comrades.

I provided dessert for everybody in the car. I had brought several pounds of caramels from America. I gave everybody in the car, including the Czech secret service officer, a caramel. But for the *Chalutzim* I had a special treat: an unopened box of American chocolates, bought in the Army's PX at Nuremberg on my way to Czechoslovakia. The chocolates were good. Like all normal youngsters the *Chalutzim* had a "sweet tooth."

"Do you know," said one of the girls, "this is the first chocolate I've tasted in six years?"

My popularity was firmly established.

The oddest person I met on the train was a twenty-one-year-old *Chassid* whose name was Lain Sholem. The *Chassidim* are a mystical religious sect who revolted against the arid formalistic ritualism of orthodox Judaism. Sholem had a thin fringe of beard, small gold-rimmed spectacles and an old man's manner.

Sholem told me he was born near Smolensk in 1925. He attended the Russian schools but after school studied with his father, who was a *Chassidic* rabbi. He worked at his trade of bookbinder in Gorki during the war and came out of Russia under the Russo-Polish repatriation agreement as the husband of a Polish wife. The wife wasn't on the train, and I suspect it was a marriage of convenience to get him out of the Soviet Union.

I asked Sholem where he wanted to go.

"Ergetz trachten," he said in Yiddish ("Somewhere where I can think").

"Do you want to go to Palestine or America?" I asked. He said it didn't matter to him.

"What do you want to be?" was my next question.

"A *shochet*" ("a kosher slaughterer"), was the answer.

It was strange to see this youngster who had been born in the middle of one of the great revolutions of world history and apparently had been untouched by it. He had the mannerism of an old-fashioned East European rabbi. When I asked a question, he would cup one hand behind his ear, though he was not deaf, and say: *"Ha, was sagt ihr, hah?"*

("What are you saying, hah?"). I asked Sholem what he thought of the Soviet Union. The look in his little eyes was that of a man who considers himself too clever to be tripped up by such dangerous questions.

"Of that," he said, "I would rather say nothing."

Ours was a long and slow journey. We stopped not only at every one-tank town, but often on sidings along the way to let faster trains pass. At 7:10 p.m. we changed trains at a town called Chocen.

In Czechoslovakia, there are many outdoor cafés on railroad station platforms. There was a very attractive one at Chocen, with gay cloths on the tables.

When our train stopped at the station, the well-dressed folk eating dinner at the station café looked up in startled surprise to see the rabble emerging from that last car and swarming across the tracks to the train for Bratislava.

On the new train we also had the last car, another third-class carriage very much like the first, and there my *Chalutz* friends, the man with the mandolin, and I again found a compartment to ourselves.

V

The youngest of the ten *Chalutzim* had the usual story to tell. The usual story on the Jewish underground in Europe was a story of suffering, tragedy, and melodramatic escape from wholesale murder. But his had an unexpectedly happy ending that gave a vicarious thrill to every one of us in that third-class railroad car crowded with refugees.

He was sixteen. I had noticed him first when I had boarded the train at Anton. Six years of danger and under-feeding hadn't helped his growth and he was about as tall as a boy of twelve. But he had an attractive fun-loving small boy's glint in his eye. Somewhere along the way he had lost four front teeth, and his jaw was bandaged. I never found out why. His name was Abram Wroclawski and he came from Lodz in Poland.

His comrades called him Avrumikel and Avrumele—diminutives for Abram—and he was obviously the "baby" and the pet of the group. We had plenty of time to talk on that all-night journey. I sat next to him in the hard-seat compartment I shared with the *Chalutzim*. I asked him where he came from and how he had managed to survive.

"I was only nine when the war came," Avrumikel told me in Yiddish. "I was a student in a Polish school. There were two hundred thousand Jews in Lodz. The Germans put us all into a ghetto and closed it up. There were seven in my family, my father and mother, two sisters, and three brothers. It was very hard to get food in the ghetto and many people died of hunger. My father died in 1942, my mother a few months later. My two older brothers died in the ghetto in 1943.

"In 1944, the Nazis liquidated the ghetto and trans-ferred those of us who were still alive to the concentra-tion camp at Auschwitz. I had a sister who was then twelve years old. *Seh haben ihr geschickt zu verbrennen*," ("They

—meaning the Germans—sent her to be burned," i.e., the gas chamber and the crematorium.)

"I was also in a group which was to be sent to the crematorium. We all suspected what was in store for us, and when we came to the death wagons which were to take us to the crematorium, I ran away. I knew I had nothing to lose and that the worst that could happen to me was to be shot as I fled. Somehow I managed to get away in the excitement. I suppose my small size was a help.

"I fled seven kilometers to Babitz, hiding in the fields and forests by day and moving by night. I was in a tough spot because the only clothes I had were my *katzet* (concentration camp) pajamas. There was no chance of getting away in those and I did not know how to get other clothes. So I had to go to another concentration camp.

"I slipped into the camp at night. There were Poles and Jews there and German political prisoners. A German communist in the camp took a liking to me. I was sick and starved and had to be kept hidden from the guards. He brought me food and saved my life.

"I couldn't be kept hidden forever. My friend went to a Jewish inmate who worked in the SS bureau at the camp. Through this Jew I obtained papers as a prisoner. There were hundreds in the camp and as long as I had these papers I could move about freely. I was just one more Jewish prisoner. I stayed there four months and was then transferred to Buchenwald.

"I spent the rest of the war in Buchenwald. We worked in nearby factories by day, usually twelve hours or more, with little to eat. Many of us died of hunger. Three days before the Americans arrived, the SS guards took forty thousand Jews out of the camp. The Jews were told that they were being transferred but those of us who were lucky enough to be left in the camp later learned that they had been taken to prepared graves in a forest not far away and shot.

"The day after that, there were rumors that the American troops were only ten kilometers away and our SS guards fled. On April 11, 1945, *halb vier* (at 3:30) I was set free. Those of us who were strong enough cheered and wept with joy. The Americans were very good to us, but some prisoners were so weak from long starvation that the liberation came too late.

"I stayed in Buchenwald two months after the liberation. I knew my father, mother, two brothers, and one sister were dead, but I thought that perhaps the other sister might still be alive. As soon as I felt strong enough to travel I wanted to go search for her. Just before the Russians took over that territory, an American officer told me I could get home on an UNRRA repatriation train to look for her. When I got back to Lodz I found her. There she is."

Avrumikel pointed to a girl who had been listening to his story with a smile. All the *Chalutzim* turned to me expectantly, to see if I shared their happy feeling. Among the refugees who had been in concentration camps, few ever found even distant relatives. To have returned home and discovered a sister was little less than a miracle. Now brother and sister were going together to Palestine.

The sister was nineteen, with bright blue eyes and dark curly hair. She was not much taller than her brother. Her name was Sarah. She too had been sent to Auschwitz from the Lodz ghetto.

"I said good-by to my little sister there and to my other friends," Sarah said, "for we all expected to be sent to the crematorium. But I was strong and old enough to work so the Germans sent me instead to Magdeburg.

"I finally went to Bergen-Belsen concentration camp. We were put to work in a German munitions factory. I was at a machine that smoothed the cases for bullets. I found it very hard to work. I would stand at the machine and cry so much that I couldn't see through my tears. I thought 'these bullets are killing the people I love' and I would cry harder.

"One day a woman foreman, a German, came to me and asked why I cried. I told her, and she showed me how without attracting attention I could spoil the bullets so they would not shoot. After that I stopped crying.

"We worked very hard on little more than thin soup and bread. It seemed that we worked day and night, marching back and forth in the darkness and cold to the concentration camp for a few hours sleep each day. Many could stand no more and just lay down and died. It seemed an endless agony, through which we passed half asleep.

"When the American troops broke into Germany and began to approach Bergen-Belsen, the German guards took us out of the camp. They said they were transferring us to another camp further in the interior. They said the Americans might shoot us. We knew that was a lie.

"When we stopped for our first rest on the road, the Germans began shooting at us from all sides. Some of us had fallen asleep alongside the road. Others just sat too weary to sleep. Many were shot running away. I was one of the lucky few who escaped.

"I got to Loburg, about forty kilometers from Magdeburg. There, on the 8th of May, 1945, I was freed by the Russians, and *ich hab bald gefahren aheim* (and I at once started traveling home)."

I asked Sarah how she traveled back to Poland and she said she made the trip on foot.

"It was quite a journey," she said with a wry smile. "There were hundreds of us on the roads, making for home.

"But when I got back to Lodz I found I had no home. The house we lived in had been burned to the ground. I could not find even distant relatives and I saw only one or two of my old friends. Most of the Poles I encountered hated the Jews more than ever.

"Then," Sarah said, *"hab ich gesehn az fur Yidden is nit tu kein ander weg* (I saw that for Jews there was no other way left open) and I entered a *kibbutz* and began to prepare myself for Palestine."

Sarah said she had not been a Zionist before the war. She entered the *kibbutz* at *Dror*. She learned Hebrew and tailoring, and it was there that her brother found her. Her brother also joined the colony. He picked chauffeuring for his trade.

"Our trade school," her brother said, "had one jeep an American soldier had given us and we all practiced on that."

The two children told me they lost one uncle in the

Warsaw ghetto and had another uncle in the Warsaw ghetto and another in New York.

"I haven't written to him," Avrumikel said, "but I'd like him to know we are on our way to *Eretz Israel* (Palestine)."

I telephoned the news to his uncle in New York when I got back.

VI

Many of the Jews who survived the Hitler period were people who passed as Aryans. There was one such person among us. She was a short, stocky blonde of twenty from Lwow, which was Polish before the war and is part of the Soviet Ukraine today. Her name was Sarah Barach and one would have taken her for a Slavic *shicksa* (gentile girl) of Polish or Ukrainian origin. This had been her salvation.

Under the German occupation, Sarah had lived in a ghetto in Lwow. When the ghetto was liquidated, Sarah and her mother were among those loaded on the death wagons bound for the gas chamber and the crematorium. Sarah jumped off the wagon along the way and escaped in the darkness after one last quick hug and kiss from her mother. The guards didn't see her, and her Aryan appearance made it easy for her to find shelter and work.

Life as an Aryan also had its hazards in that part of the

world. Lwow is Polish, but the countryside is Ukrainian. Before the war the Roman Catholic Poles treated the Uniat and Orthodox Ukrainians worse than they did the Jews. The Nazis did their best during the occupation to fan the old hatred between the Poles and the Ukrainians.

"I lived as a Pole," Sarah told me, "working as a servant girl and farmhand in the country until, late in 1942, Ukrainians began murdering Poles. I had to flee, but when I settled down again on a farm to work I said I was a Ukrainian and it was as a Ukrainian that I lived until the Russians reconquered that territory. I spoke both Polish and Ukrainian fluently.

"The only narrow escape I had was the result of a dream. I dreamed I was home with my mother. The next morning the wife of the peasant for whom I worked said: 'I heard you singing a Jewish song in your sleep last night.' I was frightened, but laughed it off. I said it was a song I had learned when I worked as a servant girl for Jews before the war."

Sarah had an odd story to tell when I asked her whether she had come across any Germans friendly to the Jews.

"While working as a Ukrainian, I once met a Wehrmacht (German Army) soldier," Sarah related. "In the course of our conversation, I said to him in broken German: 'Those Jews are no good.' His answer surprised me.

" 'Some Jews are no good,' the German soldier replied. 'But I have known some very good Jews.' And then he added a surprising sentence. He spoke simply, as to a person who didn't understand his language well. 'Hitler no good,' the Wehrmacht soldier told me. He said it like a person who had stored that thought up a long time, and was both relieved and frightened to get it off his chest."

Four of the *Chalutzim* were Polish Jews who had known life under both the Russians and the Germans. Dov Potashnick, a nineteen-year-old boy from a little Jewish town called Oszmiana near Vilna, was pointed out to me as the author of the song I heard when I first boarded the refugee train for Bratislava, *Chalutzim Greten Sich fahr Eretz Israel (Pioneers Prepare Themselves for Palestine)*. His home town was occupied by the Russians after the invasion of Poland in 1939. I asked him how he found it under the Russians.

"Ganz gut, nit schlecht (quite good, not at all bad),"* was his answer. "But in 1941 the Germans came and then our *tsoros* (sorrow) began. In a week we were all wearing yellow *Mogen Dovids* (six-pointed Jewish stars) on our arms. A month later I lost my father and elder brother when the SS surrounded our town and shot eight hundred men.

"The rest of us were put into a ghetto where I lived with my mother and sister until 1943. In 1943 the ghetto was liquidated. The last I saw of my mother and sister was when they were taken away with other women to Auschwitz, where they were gassed and burned. I was sent to a camp in Stutthoff, later to Buchenwald and then to Rhinesdorf. We were slave workers and I was one of the lucky few who survived the endless work and meager food.

"In April, 1945, with the American troops only thirty kilometers away, the Germans began to move us to a new camp in Czechoslovakia. We traveled for five days in slow freight trains, with nothing to eat but a few potatoes. On the way the train was bombed and we ran away, but the SS men recaptured about one thousand of us and marched us off on foot to Theresienstadt in Czechoslovakia. Those who couldn't stand the march were shot. Eight hundred of us arrived. I, like many others, was feverish and spotted with typhus. There, a few days later, on May 9, 1945, we were freed. I was sick for several months and then went back to Lodz, where I entered a *kibbutz* to prepare myself for life as a pioneer in Palestine."

I told Potashnick that getting to Palestine wouldn't be quite as easy as boarding a train to Bratislava, that he might have to wait months in a DP camp in Germany before he could start for Palestine, and then run a British blockade to enter.

"I'll get there," Potashnick said confidently. "Those are minor troubles after the things I've been through."

Myra Bergman, a sandy-haired slim girl of twenty-five who came from Thorn in Poland, was one of the lucky few who escaped from the German-occupied zone into the Soviet Union.

"Shortly after the Germans occupied Poland in 1939," Myra related, "all the Jews in my town were summoned to gather in the *platz* (the central square). There were six thousand of us. It was a cold, wintry evening. We were marched off on foot without baggage to Warsaw.

"During the night some of us managed to slip away. I made for the new Russian frontier (the Ribbentrop-Molotov line). A German soldier captured me on the border and cursed me. 'You must be a communist,' he shouted, 'if you're trying to get into the Soviet Union.' But when I cried and pleaded with him, he let me go over the border.

"But that was not the end of my troubles. There was a no-man's land between the German and Russian borders. I had got over the German border, but now couldn't cross the Russian. The Russians wouldn't let us in. There were several thousand Jews in that area. The snows had begun and it was bitterly cold. We had no shelter. Peasants smuggled food into the area, but at prices few could afford to pay. It cost ten *zlotys* (about $1.80) for a liter of milk.

"We were there eight days. Finally, in desperation, we stormed the Russian border, overpowered the guards and got across. We made our way to Byalostok, about sixty miles from the Ribbentrop-Molotov line. There we got help from the Jewish community.

"Shortly after we arrived," Myra said, "the Russian Government ordered the evacuation of Jewish and other refugees from that border region to the interior of the Soviet Union. The Russians were already preparing for a possible German attack. We were in the first defense zone. It is fortunate for us, though we did not know it at the time, that we were moved. Twenty thousand of us were transported on sleighs to various *kolkhozes* (collective farms) in Russia and the Ukraine."

I asked Myra how Jewish refugees were treated in the collective settlements.

"*Sehr gut aufgenommen*" (very well received)," was

her answer. "At the *kolkhoz* to which I was sent, we were greeted with a parade and a band as victims of Fascism. The people there were *sehr moralische menschen* (very moral people). We worked hard on the farm and learned manual trades."

Myra added a significant sentence about her experience before the German attack in 1941. Myra said that she and the other refugees at that *Kolkhoz* had *"gar nicht gefült wir sind Juden"* ("had not at all felt themselves Jews"), but had been made to feel at home and in no way different from the other people in the collective.

"When the Germans attacked," Myra went on, "we were again evacuated, this time to Tashkent in Asiatic Russia, north of Afghanistan. It was a terrible journey. Transport was disorganized. We had little bread to eat. Typhus broke out on the way, but we were well treated on our arrival. We worked on farms in Uzbekistan during the war, and after the war was over I went back to Poland to see if I could find any relatives. I found none.

"The reception we got in Poland was not a pleasant one. The first thing we heard when the repatriates came across the Polish border from the USSR were cries of *"zhidi kommunisti"* (Jew Communists). For those Poles we were only more Jews to kill. I don't ever want to see Poland again."

VII

I don't think I shall ever forget that first night on the train to Bratislava. There were no lights. Imagine a darkened third-class compartment for eight in which there were twelve of us: the ten *Chalutzim,* the man with the mandolin, and myself.

We halted every fifteen or twenty minutes at stations or on sidings. Once, just before midnight, we stopped at a station with a lunch stand and I bought big sugared cookies for the children—the *Chalutzim,* none of them more than in their early twenties, seemed children to me, no different from my own three at home.

It was a starry night, cool and clear, and one's eyes grew accustomed to the darkness. Outside one saw what seemed an endless procession of sleeping Czech and later Slovak farmhouses, hamlets, and small towns. The old-fashioned yellow lamps at the stations and the crossroads threw their light into the compartment as we passed them.

The man with the mandolin played and one *chaver* (comrade) after another sang. I have never heard singing that touched me so much. The songs I heard were songs that had sprung from the Nazi-created ghettoes, the concentration camps, and the forest hideouts of the Jewish Partisan bands. Many were the spontaneous creation of anonymous longing.

One of the songs I heard was a *Volkslied* (a people's

song) about a small East European village called Slutsk.
Before Hitler, there were many such Jewish villages in
Poland and the Ukraine. The song evoked memories of a
Jewish life which has passed away forever. Except for a
scattered remnant, the pious Jews who lived in those vil-
lages are dead.

The refrain of the song was *Slutsk, mein Slutsk, mein
Stadtel, ich benk nach dir* (Slutsk, my Slutsk, my little
hometown, I long for you). There were lines in it that
provided vivid glimpses of the life the young *Chalutzim*
on the train had known as children and would never see
again. One stanza pictured the village on *Erev Shabbos*
(Sabbath eve, Friday night) when the Sabbath candles
were lit and there were prayer services in the synagogue.
I remember two lines:

> *Flegt die Mama benchen*
> *Tate flegt in Beth Hamidrash gehn*
> (Mother used to bless the Sabbath candles
> (Father used to go to *Beth Hamidrash*)

The *Beth Hamidrash,* the social center of an orthodox
village, was a house used during the week for the study
of the *Torah* (Bible and Law) and for worship on holi-
days and the Sabbath.

To hear the song was to see the village peaceful with
the new Sabbath, to see the white linen and the fresh
baked *cholah* (white twisted bread) on the table, mother
saying her Sabbath prayers over the newly lit candles in
the brass seven-pronged *Menorah.* Father would be washed
and in his Sabbath best, going off with his cronies to the
Beth Hamidrash. If I, who had never known that life

could see it as I heard the singing, imagine how vivid it must have been to those who had lived it as children and were now leaving it forever!

The sixteen-year-old "baby" of the *Chalutzim*, Avrumikel, sang another ghetto song about a Jewish town. The song is called *Es brennt* and it pictures a village being burned by the Nazis: *Es brennt, bruderle, es brennt* (it is burning, little brother, it is burning). I remember one line. It went, *lescht mit eier eigen blut* (extinguish it with your own blood).

Another song, *In Sahara,* told of a dream in which one found oneself in a land of palaces with silver doors and gardens with trees from which the birds sang. The dreamer awakens in the concentration camp. The chorus was:

Es is a liegen
Es is a liegen
Es is a puster treim
Der Midbar is kein land, kein feld un kein baum.
(It is a lie
(It is a lie
(It is a futile dream
(In the desert is no land, no field and no tree.)

I heard a *lager lied* (concentration camp song) called *Treblinka. Treblinka* was the name of a concentration camp. "We used to sing it at night as we lay in the concentration camp," Avrumikel told me. "It was comforting to sing." The song is a song of lost homes and parents with a chorus which goes:

Treblinka dort
Far yeden Yid das gute ort

Wer's komt ahin
Verbleibt schon dort
Dort in Treblinka.
(Treblinka there
(For every Jew the 'Good Place'
(Who comes there
(Remains there always
(There in Treblinka.)

"Good Place" is Yiddish idiom for cemetery.

One ghetto song called *In A Lithuanian Village* told the story of a little girl whose mother places her in a Christian orphan asylum to save her life. (On the illegal boat to Palestine I was later to meet a girl of ten whose life was saved in just this way.) The child pleads with her mother, *Ich will mama gehn mit dir . . . ich will nit bleiben da allein* (I want to go with you, mother, I don't want to stay here alone).

The mother kisses and comforts her, but tells the child the orphanage must be her home if her life is to be saved. The mother sings to the child that from then on the child will never again hear:

Kein Yiddish wort,
Kein Yiddish lied,
Fun haint, mein kind,
Bist mehr kein Yid.
(No Jewish word,
(No Jewish song,
(From today on, my child,
(You are no more a Jew.)

The child pleads but the mother pushes her into the

orphanage and runs into the street *mit roite oigen fin zewain* (her eyes red with tears) and she explains in the song that like the mother of Moses she had no recourse but to put her child in strange hands, *andersh hab ich nit gekent* (I could not do otherwise.)

This is a very sentimental song. It is one thing to read in cold print, it was another to hear it sung by a girl *Chalutz* who had herself lost her mother, to hear it in a darkened train compartment rumbling across the Czechoslovak plains, in a car filled with refugees.

For these children, on their way out of Europe, the songs they sang said farewell to vanished homes and parents. Every once in a while one of the *Chalutzim* would retreat into the shadows and I would see a head bend and shoulders shake. The girls mothered each other, and the *Chalutzim* slept leaning one against the other.

Toward three in the morning, with everyone asleep, I stepped carefully over their feet and went to the back of the car. I stood watching the rails stretch out behind us in the darkness until the sky began to grow gray with the first hints of dawn.

UNDERGROUND TO PALESTINE

Through The Iron Curtain

Through the Iron Curtain

I

We reached Bratislava at 5:30 the morning after leaving Anton. It was a cold dawn and Bratislava, with its onion-shaped church towers and massive stone buildings, looked grayer than usual under that sunless sky.

The Czech secret service officer in plain clothes who was our guard and escort helped the women shoulder their bags and knapsacks as the train came into the station. We must have made an odd spectacle as we trooped out of the station and straggled down the street.

We were a sleepy-looking, unshaven, unwashed, and

ragged horde led along the streets by a sheepish-looking elderly Czech gentleman. One little boy was marching briskly along in his bare feet, his precious one pair of shoes slung over his shoulders. Near him walked the skinniest little woman I have ever seen: she looked like the pictures of people who had been starved almost to death in concentration camps. She had on only a thin dress, and shivered with cold and fatigue.

Two women carried babies. A short man strode along in a big Russian army overcoat that was meant for a much larger fellow. It fell below his ankles and sagged over his narrow shoulders. The *Chalutzim* looked drowsy and a little resentful, like children who have just been told that it's time to get up and go to school.

There were few carts or people on the streets. The first sign of color and activity was encountered when we came to newly renamed Stalinova Square.

The big square was full of peasants who had come into town with their wagons to sell their produce. They had set up makeshift stands on which were piled red cherries, white radishes, green peppers, yellow onions, fresh white cheeses, and flowers of many kinds.

On one side of the square was a melancholy looking iron-colored old church with a bulbous Byzantine tower. On the other lay our destination, the Hotel Jelen, the UNRRA repatriation center in Bratislava.

The hotel was a medieval, stone building which might once have been the town house and fastness of a Slovak nobleman. It had long passed its time of glory. The few windows in front were encrusted with dirt. It had been bombed by the Russians and a hole gaped on one side of the roof.

We went through a small door which had been cut in what was formerly a wooden entrance large enough to admit a nobleman's four-in-hand. On the right was the UNRRA office, where we awakened an elderly and querulous concierge who had been sleeping in his clothes.

In front of us, beyond the arched entrance, was a large courtyard circled by a broken balcony of iron grillwork. There was horse dung in the court. Obviously it hadn't been swept for days.

An ancient staircase of stone curved upward in a magnificent spiral just inside the grand entrance, but the steps were chipped and broken. An old mirror on the stairs mocked us with our own ragged images as we mounted to the reception room on the next floor.

We left our bags in a big room that contained a few rickety single beds and many cot mattresses on the floor. The place was filthy. The interior was bomb damaged; water had leaked in, adding one more hue to the discoloration of the unpapered walls.

The stairway walls were scrawled over with handwriting. One saw this kind of scrawl in every reception center in Europe and along the stairs in every building housing a Jewish organization. Refugees wrote their names and home towns on every wall they came to with the hope that some friend or relative might see them. Our refugees, having rid themselves of their baggage, went immediately to read the names, each trying to find someone he used to know, or perhaps a relative.

Even those who knew they had no one left joined with the others in reading along the walls—just in case; who knows? The age of miracles had not yet passed. And anyway it was thrilling to be there when a familiar name was discovered. None of our group found any names that morning.

A harassed young Jewish attendant insisted that the Czech officer and I come up to his private apartment on the third floor. It was a single room with a washstand behind a screen, a wooden table with three chairs, and an unmade cot on which he slept. We were to have breakfast with him, he said, and when he went out to shop I went downstairs to say good-by to the *Chalutzim*. They were to have their breakfast at a Joint Distribution Committee canteen.

We breakfasted on white radishes, sour cream, rye bread with butter and hot coffee. The Czech seemed as moved by what he had seen and heard on the trip from Anton as I was. When he left I thanked him for the kindness he had shown the refugees.

My next stop was to be Vienna. But I did not yet know how I or my refugee comrades would succeed in making that second leg of our journey.

II

The Jewish underground representative in Bratislava did his best to dissuade me from traveling the illegal route through the Russian zone of Austria to Vienna.

I had gone to the Hotel Carlton. I wanted a hot bath and a little time alone. I had just finished dressing and was looking out the casement window over the Balkan rooftops to the Danube when there was a knock on my door.

My visitor was a young *schliach*. His name was Isak, and he had been sent to Bratislava because he was of Slovak birth, spoke the language fluently and knew the country well. He was in his late twenties, dark eyed, with a touch of swarthiness in his skin. He looked Hungarian as do many of the Slovak Jews.

His name was on my list of underground contacts and I showed him my underground passport.

I asked how I could get to Vienna. I had a military transit visa for the French and American zones in Austria from the American military attaché in Prague, but had no clearance for the Soviet zone. Isak thought I should get an Austrian visa and take the bus to Vienna, where I could rejoin the refugees at the Rothschild Memorial Hospital. I told him I preferred to go by the illegal route.

"You'll be very uncomfortable," he said, "and you'll have to walk eight kilometers (about five miles) across the border. Why don't you take the bus and see these people again in Vienna?"

I told him I didn't mind being uncomfortable and that I didn't mind walking. I asked if he was thinking only of my comfort or if he was afraid that my presence in the illegal convoy might make trouble. I said that I didn't want to endanger the crossing but that if I would cause no embarrassment I wanted to go along.

Isak assured me he was thinking only of my comfort and that if I really wanted to travel the illegal route I was welcome. We decided it would be better, however, if I went in civilian clothes as a refugee lest the correspondent's uniform create suspicion in the Russian zone. It was arranged for me to turn up at the Hotel Jelen at one o'clock the next afternoon for the trip across the border.

After lunch I shopped. Bratislava was one of the few places in Europe where food was plentiful and unrationed. This was so even during the war when Slovakia was an "independent" state under the Nazis. The Germans used to vacation there. They called it "Schweinland," either because pork was plentiful or as a reflection on the country itself. I bought two kilos of salami and some candy to feed my *chalutz* comrades on the way to Vienna. They did not expect to see me again and I looked forward to surprising them.

Two kinds of refugees get through to Bratislava. One comes in a more or less regular way from points on the Czech-Polish border, as I had. Others cross the Slovak border from Poland and make their way to Bratislava as best they can.

My first morning in Bratislava I encountered six *Chalutzim,* three boys and three girls, who had reached Bratislava without aid of any sort. I found them on the stairs of a Jewish organization which had not yet opened for the day. One of the girls was lying on the steps crying.

I offered her some chocolate which she tearfully refused. I asked one of the others what was the matter. He told me their group had come across the Tatra mountains from Poland into Slovakia, that the girl was crying from weariness but would be all right once she had a chance to rest.

To come over the Tatras is a difficult and hazardous journey. Hiding out in those mountains were SS men, remnants of the Anders' anti-government Polish forces and renegade Red Army soldiers who had served under the turncoat Russian General Bender. They seemed to have a plentiful supply of dollars and pounds, which they spent in the villages on either side of the border.

One of the *Chalutzim* was wearing a Red army uniform and boots. His name was Schmulik Segal. He came from Grovno in what was then Poland, and had been a lieutenant in the Red Army. He said he had fought his way west with the army from Stalingrad to Lwow and then on to Vienna. He was wounded, spent four and a half months in a hospital in the Caucasus and then fought in the Russian campaign against Japan.

"When the war against Japan ended I went to Khaborovsk," Schmulik told me, "and was sent back to Moscow, where I was demobilized and given my papers back to Poland as a Polish citizen. I found no one I knew in Poland, except my brother Yankel who fought in the Polish Army. Our old home was destroyed and we entered a collective to train for Palestine."

Sometimes these unescorted tours across Slovakia did not end so well. I was packing at the hotel later that same morning when Isak arrived, very much disturbed. He said that some thirty Jewish refugees who had crossed into Slovakia from Poland had been stopped by the police about a hundred kilometers from Bratislava and were to be sent back to Poland. He asked if I could do anything to help them.

The American UNRRA chief was sympathetic. He suggested that I try to see the Minister of the Slovak Ministry of the Interior since that department controls the police. He offered me a car and the services of his Czech secretary.

In Slovakia, which has considerable autonomy within the Czechoslovak state, the government is about two-thirds Democratic and one-third Communist. The Democrats number some democratic elements but are chiefly reactionary, undemocratic, and anti-Semitic. Some of their election leaflets looked as if they might have been prepared by the Nazis.

Fortunately for the refugees, the Ministry of the Interior is in the hands of the communists. Dr. Julius Viktory, the Minister, agreed to see me. Through my Czech interpreter I told him that I was an American newspaper correspondent telling the story of the illegal Jewish emigration. I said I was impressed with the kindness the Czechs were showing to the Jews. I informed him that I had heard that morning of the case of thirty Jews who were being refused passage by the Slovak police and ordered back to Poland. I declared that I would regret having to make an unfavorable report on the treatment of Jewish refugees in Slovakia and asked what was going to be done with the detained group.

Dr. Viktory assured me that as an anti-Fascist he understood the problem facing the Jews of Eastern Europe, that he was sympathetic.

"I am sending orders to the local police," he went on, "instructing them to release the refugees and to allow them to proceed to Bratislava on their way across Slovakia to Vienna."

I thanked Dr. Viktory. I just had time to join the illegal transport for Vienna.

III

At the hotel I changed into civilian clothes, but left off my necktie to look less respectable. At the Hotel Jelen I learned that the refugees had already started for the railroad station, but I caught up with them.

At the station I found that the original fifty with whom I had traveled from Anton had been increased by two hundred more refugees who had come into Bratislava by various means and from many points on the Polish-Czechoslovak border. Four old freight cars were waiting for us. They were attached to the end of a local train and had been arranged for by UNRRA. We all climbed up in a happy mood and made ourselves as comfortable as we could. There were twenty-five children among the two hundred and fifty. The youngest, a child of three months, was being suckled by its mother when we entered our car.

The *Chalutzim* were excited to see me again. They all began talking at once. A *Haganah* worker we had not seen before came up and warned us to be quiet. He told

us that we were supposed to be natives of the country of
Z————. He said we were to speak only Hebrew, not
Yiddish. The Yiddish was recognizable because of its
high German content, but the Hebrew would sound
strange enough to pass for the language of that far country, Z————.

Our new escort was a young Hungarian Jew, an ex-
partisan who had later become a *Haganah* man, a sturdy
chap, lively and full of fun. He was very popular with
the frontier guards. He made the trip from Vienna to
Bratislava every other day, taking a party of refugees
across the border each time he returned to Austria.

He told us that so many Jews had crossed that border
as natives of Z————, all of them speaking Hebrew,
that occasional groups of Z————'s found things difficult. On one occasion a number of Z————'s arrived
at the border with authentic repatriation papers. The
guards were used to seeing the somewhat less than genuine documents carried by Jewish refugees and became
suspicious. To test the Z————'s the guards asked:

"How do you say 'good evening' in the Z————
language?"

The Z————'s all said good evening in their own
tongue.

"Aha," said the guards, "we thought there was something odd about this party. The way to say good evening
in Z———— is *erev tov.*"

Erev tov is good evening in Hebrew.

The escort spoke Hungarian, Hebrew, a little English,
but he knew no Yiddish. In his khaki shirt and trousers,

with his face tanned by the sun, and his informal manner, he could easily have passed for a typical American boy. He told us that one time when he was convoying a group of Jews pretending to be Z————'s he ran into a policeman who knew a Z———— living in that town. The policeman called the Z———— over and said:

"Here are some of your compatriots."

The Z———— began to talk in his own language. "I didn't know what to do," our escort said. "I was afraid we were in for trouble. I started talking Hebrew as fast as I could to the Z————, but I interspersed it with the name of the most northerly province of Z———— where the people speak a different dialect. I kept saying I was from that province. All he could catch was the name of the province. Finally he turned to the policeman and said: 'These are Z————'s all right, but they come from the province of X where they speak a different dialect.'

"I assure you," said the *Haganah* worker, "I was in quite a sweat by the time that conversation was over."

Three-quarters of an hour after we left Bratislava we reached the end of the line in Slovakia. We got off at a small station about four kilometers from the border. Our *schliach* led us quickly out of the station by a side gate before any questions could be asked, and down a dusty road in the hot afternoon sun. Near me marched a young mother, barefoot, with her baby tied to her back papoose fashion. At one point a few ducks joined the procession and waddled along in great dignity beside us.

We stopped beside a brook where there was a patch

of grass and trees. There we all put down our bags and rested while the *schliach* dickered with a peasant for two carts to carry the bags, the children and the sick. We were all supposed to chip in to pay the cost but it took a lot of scolding by the *Haganah* man to make some of the refugees part with a contribution from their meager funds.

Most of us stretched out for a rest on the grass while we waited. A half dozen peasant children and two gypsies looked on curiously. Two peasant women, their skirts rolled up, went on calmly washing clothes in the nearby brook.

When the *schliach* finally finished haggling with the peasant, the carts were loaded and forded across the brook. We marched across single file over a narrow wooden plank and formed in rows of five on the other side for our march to the border.

I must say a word about our luggage, which was the oddest assortment of knapsacks, handbags, paper bags, burlap bags, and old suitcases I have ever seen. The luggage was no stranger than we were. In the front row, as we began to march forward, was an old grandfather with a beard. He had an extra pair of shoes hanging over his shoulder. In the rear was a very fat woman who limped along in ill-fitting shoes and carried an ancient black umbrella as a parasol against the sun. Most of us had two loaves of bread each slung over our shoulders, these being the principal rations handed out at the Hotel Jelen for our journey.

Ahead of us was a small village. We started down the dusty main street in silence. Dogs began barking as we went by. Geese honked and roosters crowed, a cow ambled down a side street and stood watching us placidly as we went by. An elderly peasant sat outside his house peacefully smoking a long pipe. A kind-hearted peasant woman began to pump at a well along the street and offered us water. Many broke ranks to have a drink.

It was very hot, but many of us wore not only coats but all the belongings we could possibly wear, as one way of carrying them across the border. I had on a shabby blue raincoat to hide my too respectable looking brown tweed suit.

Sweat poured from us. The gravel crunched beneath our feet. I don't think I shall ever forget that steady tramp, tramp, tramp as we marched toward the border.

We soon left the village and proceeded over a rough stone causeway to the Czech-Austrian frontier barrier. On the left were mountains. On the right cows grazed in a sunken meadow. The children grinned happily from the top of the luggage piled in the two carts at the head of the procession, which came to a halt at the gates.

IV

On the other side of the barrier on the Czech-Austrian border was a long bridge across what seemed to be an extensive marsh, with a sluggish river running through it. Three Czech officers sat on the railing. Although this was the boundary of the Russian zone of Austria, no Russians or Austrians were in sight.

This is the way we got across: Our Hungarian friend had a list of all us Z————'s on official looking stationery. As he read each name the person whose name was called would answer and run across the border. The names were typically Jewish—Rosenblum, Yacob; Adler, Rifkah; Abramovitch, Itzik—and these created a good deal of amusement among the Czech officers lounging on the railing, because they knew that these were hardly the names of Z————'s.

A cool breeze blew over the frontier bridge as we waited. The Hungarian *schliach* was supposed to call out my name at some point, as though I too were on the list. I waited until about two-thirds of the refugees had gone over, growing more and more restless. I was afraid he might have forgotten me. When he called out "Bromov, Moishe," and no Moishe Bromov answered, I seized the opportunity. I ran up to the border, said I was Moishe Bromov, and passed over to the other side. I never found out what happened to the real Moishe Bromov.

When we had all gotten across, we proceeded with our march. This passage through Mr. Churchill's "iron curtain" was the easiest frontier crossing on my entire trip. We seemed to have stirred little curiosity on the Russian side.

Our first contact with the Russians occurred when we made way for a Russian officer riding by on horseback. At one point we passed a playing field where Russian soldiers were playing English-style football. Two carriages passed us, with Russian soldiers and their fraülein friends out for a gay afternoon. Near the railroad station on the Austrian side, a group of Russian soldiers and officers stood along the road to watch us go by, but no questions were asked.

About four kilometers from the border, we arrived at a railroad station, where our bags were unloaded and we picked them up and crowded into third-class carriages, headed for Vienna. It was about four o'clock in the afternoon.

For some reason, perhaps out of the misguided notion that I preferred to travel with the better element, the *schliach* ushered me up to the first third-class carriage where he saw to it that the one obviously well-to-do refugee family and I had a whole compartment to ourselves. I was annoyed because I really wanted to be with my *Chalutzim.*

The head of the prosperous family was a pretentious Polish Jew who wore a good suit of clothes, pince-nez glasses and a pompous air. He had once been to America and imagined that he could speak English, which he would attempt to do with the slightest encouragement. His buxom wife assumed the expression of a lady who wanted everyone to understand that she might swoon at any moment. Somehow she had managed to get to the border with a wrist watch and three diamond rings. On her feet she wore a huge pair of high men's shoes, black and dirty, with round stubbed toes of the kind one usually associates with stevedores. With these two *pritzim* (Yiddish slang for would-be aristocrats) was their well dressed, pretty daughter, who was accompanied by her youn husband.

Before the train started I stuck my head out of th window and waved frantically to attract the attention o the *Chalutzim*. Two of them ran up to join me. I hac missed lunch because of my interview with the Sloval minister. We got out the salami and a penknife. Th *Chalutzim* had a big loaf of bread and we started to eat I could see that the mouths of our dignified friends wer watering and offered them salami. They all accepted ex cept the mother, who looked as if she wouldn't think o eating any such horrible stuff, especially when it was cu by a dirty penknife.

At every stop, and there were many, more *Chalutzim* ran up to join me and the salami. The lady was horrifiec by my disreputable friends.

At 5:15 we changed trains at Ganserndorf. The statior had been badly bombed. Here we lost the luxury of ou third-class compartment and were packed in among a lo of annoyed Austrian peasants and working people. I sa on my bags in the vestibule. There must have been eigh of us squeezed in with our bags on that little platform.

Near me stood an elderly, haggard little hunchback He was dirty and very weary. He was about five feet tal and wore a Russian workman's cap. I didn't know whethe he was an Austrian workman or a Jewish refugee and asked one of the other passengers if he was "one of us." I was told he was. I took the remains of my salami out o my bag, cut off a thick slice and offered it to him with a piece of bread. He thanked me in Yiddish and put the food carefully away in his bag to eat later. We began talking; he told me he was a Polish Jew who had been in Russia during the war. He had worked as a postman among the collective settlements in the countryside.

Almost every refugee carries, hidden away on him like some precious possession, a grubby notebook in which he has the names and addresses of relatives and friends, and he will ask if you know so and so in "Chicago" and "Neff York." The little hunchback was no exception.

His name was Schloime Weisman and he came from Brok nach Bugiem in Poland. He wanted to know whether I knew a Rabbi Jacob M. Pomerance. The only address he had for him was Brooklyn 6, New York. I told him I didn't. He then confided that the rabbi and he had gone to the same theological seminary.

"What did you do before the war?" I asked Weisman.

"Gelernt" ("studied"), was the answer.

The one word carried a world of satisfaction. He had been in a *Yeshivah* (theological seminary) when the war began.

"Hard work," he added, ironically.

"Where are you headed now?" I wanted to know.

The tired face lit up with a happy smile.

"Eretz" ("Palestine").

After much coaxing I got him to take my seat on the bag. I climbed outside the train onto the roof, which was cool and comfortable provided one kept an eye out for the low bridges.

On the roof with me was a seventeen-year-old *Chalutz* from Poland, a boy with glasses and a thin, intellectual

face. He told me he and his parents had come from Russia
and that he had left them behind to go to Palestine.

"Look," he said to me, pointing proudly. "I have this
jacket, this shirt, these pants, socks, and shoes. I brought
nothing more."

"Well," I said, "I've got a lot of shirts in my bag and
the darned thing's too full. How about taking a couple
of my shirts?"

"No," he said, with a grand gesture. "A *Chalutz* needs
nothing."

When I told him I had been to Palestine the year
before he insisted that I tell him about the colonies.

So we entered Vienna. We got off the train at Floridsdorf near one of the groups of workers' apartments which
had been shelled by Dollfuss and had never been repaired.

There, before the startled eyes of a group of Austrian
workmen, we were lined up and marched off quickly to a
corner where our Hungarian *schliach* jammed us into two
trolley cars linked together. The trolleys took us from the
Russian to the American zone.

V

Vienna reminded me of an American ghost town of
vast dimensions. It was not as badly damaged as the German cities I had seen, but the damage here seemed spiritual
as well as physical. Munich and Nuremberg could be

rebuilt in a quarter-century, but one had the feeling that the harm done Vienna was irreparable, that it would never emerge from its lesser ruins.

The scarred workers' homes we first saw at Floridsdorf were more than the wreckage of a co-operative venture in public housing—they represented the end of what was once one of the most promising working-class movements in Europe. The bomb-mangled splendor of the Ring, the famous boulevard that encircles inner Vienna, already had the aspect of a museum exhibit. The Ring is the heart of a vanished empire that seems remarkably benevolent and well ordered in retrospect. The peoples over which the Hapsburgs once ruled are poisoned by mutual hatreds: Czech against Slovak, Pole against Czech, Slovak against Maygar, Croat against Serb.

To stand in the cool of an early morning in the green park of the Rathausplatz, the city hall plaza, and look toward the delicate spires of the Votivkirche—the church the Emperor Franz Josef built in gratitude for his escape from assassination — is to get a glimpse of battered Vienna's one-time imperial splendor. It is somewhat over-adorned and not quite in the best taste, but massively impressive. In front of the vast Hofburg palace, a small imitation Greek temple carries an inscription which still proclaims, in a small quaint voice: *"Justitia Regnorum Fundamentum"* ("Justice is the foundation of kingdoms"). Nearby, on the Ring, covering part of the front of the national school headquarters, huge pictures of Lenin and Stalin proclaim a new order beyond the wildest night-mares of Franz Josef.

Opposite the Parliament House with its white angels and black horses, which looks a little as though it had been designed by a pastry cook, one can see the graves of nine Red Army heroes in the Volksgarten. At seven in the morning, many Viennese were already sitting amid the deep shade and singing birds. There were floral wreaths at the base of the monuments on the Russian graves, several of which carried pictures of the departed. The strange-looking Russian characters noted that they fell in the struggle against Fascism.

This Vienna, which begins to seem more a relic than a living city despite the trams and hurrying people in the streets, is the great crossroads of the Jewish exodus from Central and Eastern Europe, an exodus that is greater in magnitude, misery, and drama than those from Egypt and Spain.

The center of Jewish life in Vienna today is the huge Rothschild Memorial Hospital. Its squalor and vitality contrast with the faded loveliness of the city. When we marched up, the sidewalk and the steps were crowded with refugees waiting to greet any friends, relatives, or comrades they might find among the newcomers. There were cries of joy, kisses and hugs, when some of those waiting recognized people they knew in our group.

The hospital was bombed during the war and has yet to be completely repaired. It would be a rather gloomy, cavernous place were it not for the people who mill about in the corridors and stroll in the inner courtyard, gossiping cheerfully in Yiddish. Once arrived at the Rothschild Hospital, refugees feel themselves in friendly territory.

We were shepherded through the crowds and down a dark staircase into a basement full of people. We passed rooms used as a trades school and as repair shops for shoes and clothing into a large room for our medical examinations. After the medical examination we had to fill out an Army DP registration questionnaire. Among other things this recorded "Claimed Nationality," "Religion (optional)," "Last Permanent Residence or Residence January 1, 1938," "Desired Destination," "Usual Trade, Occupation or Profession," and "Languages Spoken in Order of Fluency." When this had been filled out each refugee received an identity card, with a name and number.

It is difficult for Americans, accustomed to move freely without passports through most of North America, to appreciate what it means to get this document. In Europe today even legal travelers must have papers of many different kinds. The need for "papieren" clogs the wheels of commerce and makes business in Europe an exasperating affair for businessmen.

To march across borders illegally, stateless and homeless, without documents, and then to come at last to a place where one meets a friendly reception, where one is given an identity card, is something only a refugee can fully appreciate. One suddenly becomes a person, with a name, a number, and a *paper*. One now has a right to move freely in the American zone of Austria. This privilege and this blessing the Jewish refugee owes to the American occupying forces. In spite of the complaints and occasional clashes between DP's and the military police, the United States Army is the best friend the Jewish people have in Europe today. I cannot speak too highly of the efficiency and the kindness with which General Mark Clark and Brigadier General Ralph H. Tate, deputy commanding general of the United States Forces in Austria, treat refugees coming out of Eastern Europe.

In the corridors of the Rothschild Hospital were Jews from Rumania, Hungary, Slovakia, Greece, and Yugoslavia as well as Poland. I also spoke there one evening with a small delegation representing the Jews of Vienna. These alone seemed pathetic. Before the war there were two hundrd thousand Jews in Vienna. The Hapsburgs were tolerant monarchs. Jews played a great part in the life of the city. Many were converted to Catholicism. The Jews were important in the city's cultural as well as its business life. The delegation, all elderly and gentle folk, told me there were twenty thousand Jews and half-Jews, including the Catholic Jews, left in Vienna.

Of these twenty thousand, only four thousand are people both of whose parents were Jewish and who count themselves as of the Jewish faith. More than half of the four thousand are over forty-five years of age.

"There are few young people left and these are emigrating," one member of the delegation told me. "We who remain are folk too old to begin life again somewhere else. We love Vienna, but there will soon be no Jews left in it. Anti-Semitism grew very strong under the Nazis and during the war, and there is no future here for the younger people."

For me, the most fascinating place in Vienna was the Jewish soldiers' club. It seemed to be the one place in the

capital where the Jewish officers and men of the four
occupying powers meet socially.

I met a big strapping fellow there in a Scotch High-
lander uniform who had enlisted in the British Army at
the beginning of the war and been assigned to a Scotch
regiment. He was a *sabrah. Sabrah* means cactus in
Hebrew; it is the slang term applied to denote native-born
Palestinians; they are supposed to be like the cactus, prickly
without but sweet within.

I heard an American lieutenant having a typical GI
argument in Brooklyn Yiddish with a Red Army officer
who spoke Litvak Yiddish. The American wanted to know
why the Russian soldiers weren't cleaner and better
dressed. The Russian retorted angrily that his comrades
had been fighting a war on inadequate resources and
under conditions that did not allow them to dress up.

"Our men," he concluded nastily, "didn't come here to
fraternize with fraüleins."

The Russian Jewish soldiers were intensely interested
in Palestine. One Red Army major asked many questions
about my trip to Palestine the year before.

"I'm a communist. I'm not a Zionist. But we must
support the building of Palestine. For many Jews in
Eastern Europe west of the Soviet border there is no other
way out," he said.

Another repeated to me with pride the famous remark
made by the Soviet Union's former Ambassador to Britain,
Maisky, who commented after a visit to the Jewish collective settlements in the Holy Land, "We have reached
socialism, but you have already achieved communism."

VI

The Rothschild Memorial Hospital was run by a combination of three agencies, the DP division of USFA, UNRRA, and a Jewish committee representing the DP's themselves, with aid from the American Jewish Joint Distribution Committee.

This committee was headed by a Polish Jew named Teicholz, a vigorous, cheerful man in his middle thirties of considerable executive capacity. I first met him on the Orient Express from Paris on my way to Stuttgart, two weeks before I got to Czechoslovakia. He was a leader of the Jewish resistance movement in Hungary and was part of the network which helped Jews to escape from Hitler-occupied Europe.

He told me one of the rare stories I heard of Germans helping Jews during the war. He was once captured by SS men on the Hungarian border. He had false Aryan papers but the SS suspected he was a Jew. A Wehrmacht doctor came along and said he would examine Teicholz to see whether or not he was circumcized. (Circumcision among Gentiles is far less common in Europe than in America.)

"The doctor took me into a hut on the border," Teicholz related. "He saw that I was circumcized, but he picked up the phone to the frontier station nearby and said, 'This man is an Aryan'."

"Did the doctor say anything to you?" I asked.

"All he did was shake my hand as I went out," Teicholz told me. "He was an elderly man with a sensitive face. He saved my life. The SS men sent me with the Aryan prisoners to a work camp from which I later escaped. Otherwise I would have gone with other Jews to the gas chamber. Jews caught on the border didn't have a chance."

At a concert and entertainment given by the DP's at Rothschild Hospital I met a man who had worked with Teicholz in the underground. He was a Red Army officer with three medals: the Stalin medal, and the Budapest and Vienna medals. He was a slim young man with tanned features and blue eyes and he told me that he had recently been demoted to *Unteroffizier.* He had been in charge of a concentration camp in Czechoslovakia for captured SS men. There were twenty-five hundred SS men in his camp, and he and the sixty soldiers under him had killed every one of the twenty-five hundred in two weeks. His punishment was the demotion, but he did not look as though he regretted it.

He was a Russian Jew who had been dropped by parachute on Hungarian territory in 1942 to organize partisan bands. On the side he helped the Jewish underground. The Red Army trained him carefully for this mission. He spoke both Hungarian and German and had false papers and false uniforms. He operated as an SS man and as an Hungarian army officer. The stories he told sounded incredible, but Teicholz assured me they were true.

"On one occasion," the Red Army man said, "I walked into a concentration camp in SS uniform, picked out six

Jews, said 'I want those blankety blank Jews for a purpose they won't like at all' and took them out of the
camp. When we got away I turned them over to the Jewish underground, which succeeded in smuggling them out
of the country to allied territory."

He was a patriotic Russian and I saw tears in his eyes
at the concert when one artist sang a Russian Yiddish
song:

> *Ich benk nach mein Russische heim,*
> *Nach meine Russische bruder*
> *Nach meine herzliche Russische lieder*
> (I long for my Russian home,
> (For my Russian brothers
> (For my heart-warming Russian songs.)

He called himself a Zionist and said he was strongly
in favor of helping to build up Palestine as a home for
the Jews of Central and Eastern Europe.

I met a non-Jewish illegal immigrant to Palestine in
Teicholz's office at the hospital. She was a short, dumpy,
middle-aged woman, a Pole from Galicia. Her name had
been Franciska Lorzy but she had changed it to Clara
Plitzer, a Jewish name. She was the widow of a farm
laborer, a good-hearted motherly woman.

During the war she had saved two Jewish boys from the
Nazis. Both were sons of Jewish friends. When these
friends were sent into the ghetto by the Nazis in 1941
the boys were left in her keeping. One was five, the other
four. The Germans killed both parents. After the war the
older boy was taken by the Jewish community to be

trained as a *Chalutz*. The younger one, now eight years old, was with her; she had refused to give him up.

"I told them I didn't mind his becoming a *Chalutz* and going to Palestine," she said, "but he's all I have left in the world and I'm going with him."

She took the boy's last name as her own and adopted the name Clara because she thought it sounded more Jewish than Franciska. She had been granted an illegal immigration certificate by the underground.

VII

I checked in at the Weisse Hahn, the press camp of the U. S. Forces in Austria, and got into touch with a *Haganah* representative. I was told to be ready to leave in twenty-four hours. Word had come that I was to fly back to France, where another underground agent would take me to a seacoast from which an illegal ship was scheduled to sail within a short time.

The *Chalutzim* with whom I had traveled from Bratislava had been transferred from the Rothschild Memorial Hospital to a hostel on the Alserbachstrasse. I went there to say good-by to them before leaving. A radio was blaring away in the inner courtyard when I got there and refugees were busily at work repaving the court with bricks. The hostel held about 5,000 refugees and in an upstairs barracks I received a joyful welcome from my young comrades.

They introduced me to ten other comrades from their group at the *Kibbutz Dror* in Poland who had arrived a few days ahead of them. They did not know at that time whether they were to be distributed with other refugees to camps in the American zones of Austria and Germany, or whether as *Chalutzim* they were to be smuggled over the border into a neighboring country for transportation to Palestine. To go to the camps meant a long wait, while the interminable negotiations went on between Britain and America for their admission to Palestine. To go over the border by certain mountain passes known to the underground was to have a chance to reach Palestine within a few weeks or months by illegal ship.

I warned my young friends that they might have a long wait and urged them to keep their spirits up if they found themselves in a German or Austrian DP camp. I asked them to write me, and our leave-taking was rather tearful all around. I later heard that they were among the fortunate who went ahead and that they reached Palestine safely.

My plane out of Vienna was grounded by engine trouble in Salzburg, in as lovely an airfield as I have ever seen, a bowl among the Austrian Alps. There I telephoned Leon D. Fisher, a young New Yorker who works for the Joint Distribution Committee in Salzburg. He is a professional social worker and psychiatrist.

He picked me up at the airport in a jeep and told me about the work and the camps in the American zone. The model camp of the area, and probably the one place in the world where Jewish or any other refugees really have uxurious surroundings, was at Bad Gastein, a famous vatering place where the Army took over five large hotels o house DP's.

There were fourteen hundred refugees at Bad Gastein. Camp New Palestine in Salzburg, which housed four undred and fifty people, was the next best known hostel. The largest camp was Bindermichel, which has twenty-our hundred people. About two hundred refugees are iilleted in private homes in Salzburg. There are accommo-lations for two hundred at the transient camp in Enns.

One hundred and fifty tubercular DP's were being ared for at a hospital in the American zone.

The Jewish population in the American zone in Austria iad increased from fifteen thousand to over thirty-four housand. Three thousand were in the British zone and ine thousand in the French. Conditions were good in the atter, although food was scarce.

A DP in Salzburg said that he was one of a group of ighty Jews from Poland, Hungary, and Rumania who iad made their way across Austria. They had no diffi-ulties in the Russian zone, but at Furstenfeld, in the inglish zone, they were stopped and four of their number rrested. The rest refused to go on until the four were eleased. Late in the afternoon they demonstrated outside he British headquarters; soldiers with bayonets fired guns ver their heads to stop them, and arrested four more.

"In the British prison," one man related, "I found an S Oberstürmführer and nine Jews who had been taken rom a previous illegal transport of a hundred and seventy. Ve were questioned about the illegal immigration.

"The British wanted to know how we got across the border, who led us across, how we made contact with the underground, and many other things. We told them nothing. Finally they released us."

Fisher told me that the work of the Joint Distribution Committee in caring for refugees around Salzburg was greatly helped by the friendly attitude of the Forty-Second Division under General Harry Collins. He especially praised the DP section of the Forty-Second, which was under Major A. D. Schutz.

New Palestine, in the shadow of the Alps on the outskirts of Salzburg, looked like a model village housing development. During the occupation it was an SS troop residence. Now the Jewish flag, the blue and white *Mogen Dovid* of Palestine and the Zionist movement, flies over the settlement.

Fisher was particularly proud of a Jewish children's home at St. Gilgen, high up in the Austrian Alps. We drove out to see it, past Ribbentrop's summer home. The countryside was unbelievably beautiful.

We passed a chain of aquamarine lakes set like jewels amid the green, grizzly bear mountains. There is an officers' rest camp at nearby Frischl.

The children's home was a wealthy Nazi's villa. It is high up on a mountainside and overlooks one of the lakes. Fifty children from various DP camps in Austria spend two weeks each at the home. One of the youngsters confided that he wanted to be a newspaperman. I gave him my Palestinian press card, which bore the date of my first visit to Palestine in 1945 and was printed in English, Arabic and Hebrew.

"Now," I said, "you can go to Palestine legally as a newspaperman."

The other children crowded around to see this memento of the Holy Land.

The next morning a Red Cross executive with whom I was traveling borrowed a jeep and we crossed the Austrian border to Berchtesgaden to see Hitler's hideaway.

The countryside through which we drove was Wagnerian in its lofty, turgid beauty.

The Hitler house was a wreck. Allied bombers and souvenvir hunters had left little behind them. The walls were covered with the handwriting of GI's and the *Mogen Dovids* of American Jewish soldiers. On the second floor, in the huge victory hall, the whole side of one wall had held one great window overlooking the Alps. The view made megalomania almost inescapable for anyone who lived there. Solemnly I committed a primitive act of contempt.

On the way back we passed an SS prisoners' camp with a double row of barbed wire, watchtowers, and searchlights. SS men were stretched out enjoying a sunbath.

"As far as they're concerned," said the Red Cross man, "it's an ideal place in which to relax and plan for the future."

UNDERGROUND TO PALESTINE →

Adventure in Italy

Adventure In Italy

I

I flew to X——— from Salzburg and out again in twenty-four hours. I was told that an illegal ship, the *Haganah*, was to leave a south European port within a matter of hours.

I was given a hilarious welcome when I arrived. The crew members I had seen on that memorable night back home thumped me on the back and shouted "Izzy, we knew you'd make it." They assigned me a bunk in the officers' cabin, and one of the boys loaned me an old pair of dungarees to wear on deck.

But the *Aliyah Beth* timetable had again gone awry.

There were mysterious delays. There were whispers among the crew that difficulties had cropped up on a high level. The ex-Mufti had just escaped from Paris and there was speculation that our delay was somehow connected with that escape.

I spent some time visiting the training centers for illegal immigrants in the neighborhood. In these were classes in farming, various manual trades and Hebrew—for Hebrew is the principal language of the Jews in Palestine.

One *hachsharah* (training camp) was nothing more than a miserable collection of barracks behind barbed wire which had been used as a detention camp for German prisoners of war. Others were makeshift quarters in little fishing settlements along the sea. The prize of the lot was in an ex-collaborator's villa, high up on a mountain overlooking the seacoast. Here I talked and swam with *Chalutzim* from almost every country in Europe, and I was later to travel with many of them to Palestine.

These visits were pleasant, but as day followed day with no prospect of sailing, I grew impatient. I began to be afraid that my newspaper would call me home before I completed the journey. One Sunday morning a worker of the *Haganah* arrived with the news that a refugee ship would leave a small port in Italy the following Tuesday night.

Fortunately I had a visa. I was told how I could contact the underground in that port.

When I arrived at N——— I checked in at a hotel and made for the waterfront. The ship was the *Sir Josiah Wedgewood,* a sister ship of the one I had just left. It was named for a famous champion of Zionism in the British Labor Party, a man who suggested to Jewish leaders long before the war that they ignore British immigration restrictions and take *Chalutzim* illegally to Palestine.

The *Haganah* and the *Sir Josiah Wedgewood* were 750-ton ships, formerly in the Canadian Navy. Both ships have since been captured by the British, while taking immigrants to Palestine.

I did not locate the *Sir Josiah* until I found an Italian workingman who understood enough French to lead me to the ship.

A gangplank led at a rather dizzy incline from the wharf to the stern deck of the boat. A thin faced boy in glasses whom I had met in the United States stood on guard to prevent strangers from going aboard. I recognized Jay at once, but he didn't recognize me.

I was wearing a Basque beret which I had acquired under hypnotic suggestion from a gifted salesman several days earlier, a Turkish-born French Jew known to the Americans as Joe. I wore the beret with civilian clothes in Italy and there I was taken for a Frenchman.

Since the beret seemed to have confused Jay, too, I thought I'd have some fun at his expense. Like many practical jokes, this one almost ended badly.

I walked around the wharf, looking the boat over with what was intended to be a knowing expression. I said, in what I hoped would sound like French to Brooklyn-bred ears:

"Un étrange bateau, un étrange bateau."

The sentry was worried.

I asked: *"Ou est le Capitaine?"*

The captain, I learned later, was listening from the deck but said nothing.

"Who wants to see him?" the sentry asked in English.

I didn't answer. I started walking up the gangplank. Jay stopped me and asked angrily:

"Who are you? What's your name?"

I said my name was Jacques Pirandel and added that I was from the *Deuxième Bureau.* The *Deuxième Bureau* is the FBI of France.

The sentry looked a little green around the gills.

My *Haganah* contact had instructed me to ask for any one of three people when I found the ship in N————. One was the captain, whom I had met in America. The other two were Giacomo and Pietro.

Pietro is the name of a *Haganah* worker. Giacomo is a former Partisan leader who has been very helpful to Jewish refugees. When I asked for Giacomo the sentry took me to his house near the waterfront.

My beret and bad French worried Giacomo, too, and he marched me back to the boat. Near the boat were waterfront saloons in which some of Giacomo's former Partisan followers passed much of their time in order to keep a protective eye on any illegal Jewish boats that happened to be in the harbor.

I was beginning to be worried. I had expected to be recognized sooner. I didn't want to start by giving everybody a bad fright and getting in wrong with the crew and their underground friends. I didn't know until afterwards that I might also have been in for some rough third degree from Giacomo's waterfront gang. On the way back we met another crew member who wanted to know just why I was interested in that boat.

"I'll show you what my interest is," I said, and burst out laughing. I pulled out a *PM* reporter's card with my name on it. The crew member was a *PM* reader and he laughed too. The matter was explained to Giacomo and I was allowed on board. Of course the crew members insisted:

"We knew it was you all the time."

I got to know Giacomo well. He had once been a seaman, and like many seamen he was very well read. He had quite a library, which he showed me proudly. Conrad and Jack London were two of his favorites and I gave him a copy of "Moby Dick" before I left.

I was to have an exciting adventure in this ancient seafaring town.

I had two companions. One was a gentle, slender, darkhaired woman who was the widow of a gifted Italian Jew who had emigrated to Palestine in the early twenties and become one of the most inspiring leaders the Zionist movement has known. I met American boys later, on one of the illegal ships, who told me that they had once heard him speak and that it was for them an unforgettable experience.

He was captured and executed by the Nazis during the war when he was parachuted behind the German lines in Italy. After the war his widow went to Italy to try to find some trace of relatives. I had written her in Rome asking her to join me as Italian translator.

My other companion was a man known locally as Phil. He was of medium height with a strong face, graying hair and a resourceful manner. Phil came up to me in the lobby of the hotel shortly after I arrived and before I quite knew what I was doing I had hired him as a second translator and general handyman. He spoke virtually all the East and Central European languages I was to encounter among the refugees, and assured me that he could make himself generally useful. This was no idle sales talk, as events were to show.

I had been told to keep away from the ship the day after my arrival, but to come with my companions to Giacomo's house at seven the next night.

With Giacomo were two of his Partisan followers and the chief *schliach* called Pietro. We went down to the harbor and waited for the boat to sail.

The Partisans seemed to be upset about some last-minute difficulties, but at 8 P.M. the ship began to move out of the harbor.

I was to sail on that boat. But it had been feared that if I boarded the ship in the town it might arouse suspicion since no passengers were mentioned in her clearance papers. The plan, then, called for my going aboard later that night at a point farther down the Italian shore, about fifty kilometers from the town. There the ship was to pick up twelve hundred *Chalutzim* and I was to embark with them.

In the meantime Mrs. A———, Phil, and I went sightseeing while Giacomo and the *schliach* started off to the appointed rendezvous by a route of their own. Our pur-

pose in sightseeing was to throw the police off our trail
in case we were being shadowed. I took Mrs. A——— and
Phil to see a medieval alley I had discovered earlier in the
day. The alley, its high, almost windowless dwellings still
inhabited, bore the name *Vico della Crema, gia Vico dei
Giudei* (Cream Alley, Formerly the Alley of the Jews).
It had been the ghetto of the city in the Middle Ages.

We drove from the ghetto to a nearby town, in a car
I had hired. There we had a leisurely dinner in an open
garden and came back along a narrow winding road where
we could easily see if anyone was following us. Apparently
no one was.

We parked about a block from my hotel. I walked to
the hotel, got my bags, paid my bill and hurried back to
the car. We speeded through the town, out the ancient
Aurelian way, the Roman road still in use along the narrow and precipitous coast.

About fifty kilometers from the town we came to a
lonely strip of beach. We parked in the sand and got out
in the darkness. At this point there was an inlet deep
enough to admit a large boat. There the ship was to pick
up its passengers, and there we found Giacomo and the
Haganah worker.

II

It was shortly after midnight. Behind us, rising cliff-like
from the narrow road along the beach, were the moun-

tains of the Riviera, huge dark shapes against the sky. There were no lights along the road. All we had to see by was the faint glow of a cloudless, starry sky. We sat down to wait.

Shortly before one o'clock in the morning, far out to sea, we saw a tiny triangle of light moving toward us. The triangle was made up of three lights, one red, one green, one white; the fore, aft, and port lights of a ship moving in toward shore.

Slowly the triangle grew larger, but the ship remained invisible. It looked as if a ghost ship were moving slowly toward the beach.

About fifteen minutes later we saw a long line of twelve double headlights winding its way along the coast to the south of us.

"That," the *schliach* said, "must be the first convoy."

Pietro said that two convoys of twelve trucks each were to bring twelve hundred *Chalutzim* for the embarkation. The first convoy had been scheduled to arrive at 1:00 in the morning, the second at 1:30. The ship was to come in and put down its gangplank at 1:00.

The five of us stood on the beach waiting. The *schliach* was signaling in Morse code to the boat with a flashlight. But for some reason the boat did not come into the inlet as planned.

The truck drove off in the darkness behind us. The *Chalutzim* quickly and quietly jumped off and ran down to wait on the shore. The twelve trucks drove rapidly away.

There was no noise but the crunch of gravel under hurrying feet. None of the *Chalutzim* spoke. When I walked over and whispered *Sholom,* my only greeting was an angry glare.

An hour passed with no sign of the other trucks. The boat remained about two hundred yards off shore.

I still don't know what caused the ship's delay, but knowing its officers I was not too surprised. For that ship was manned by about as odd a collection of seamen as ever sailed the seas. The oddest was an old man with a beard, a Jewish hobo who had become a member of Jehovah's Witnesses. The captain and the first mate were professional sailors, and both were ex-Wobblies. They were buddies of many sea voyages and they had the unmistakable flavor of the old IWW—militant and individualistic.

The first mate was one of the seamen who pulled the *Swastika* off the Bremen in New York harbor in 1935.

Like many of the sailors I was to meet on these illegal ships, neither of these officers was Jewish by anything but the accident of birth. They had little Jewish upbringing and no Jewish education, and were, of course, not at all religious. But they had left families in America and taken the risk of long sentences in British prisons if caught. They said they were "sore as a —— boil" about the treatment the Jews had received in Europe. They spoke a thick Brooklynese, heavily seasoned with favorite GI expletives. But their boat was shipshape and their rather conglomerate crew was well disciplined and obviously scared to death of them.

"We'll make sailors of these —— landlubbers yet," the captain proudly told me. But I suspected that it would not be easy to tell the captain what to do, and so I was not too surprised when the ship failed to come into the inlet at the scheduled time.

The *schliach* could swear very competently in half a dozen languages, too. He was furious. Giacomo was getting more and more angry and nervous. He was nervous because of the appearance along that stretch of coast of several small Italian fishing boats. These boats used searchlights for night fishing. The fish are attracted by the lights and come to the surface where they can easily be caught.

Sooner or later the fishermen could not help but become aware that something strange was going on that night on the beach. Even in the dim starlight one could see the dark forms of the *Chalutzim* huddled together like a herd of seals on the shore. Anyone could see that a flashlight was signaling in code and being answered from a big boat off shore.

Finally, about three in the morning, the boat moved in, and after some angry shouting between the *schliach* and the captain it drifted slowly into the inlet and dropped its gangplank. The gangplank consisted of two long, heavy boards, one higher than the other. The *Chalutzim* were to walk in the dark up that dizzy, uneven incline to the deck.

But at the very moment the gangplank was dropped six *carabinieri* (Italian police) sprang toward us in the darkness, shouting *"Ragazzi, Ebrie!"* or "Hey, fellas, here are a bunch of Jews!"

III

The six Italian gendarmes descended on us just as the first *Chalutzim* were about to board the boat.

We were scared. We thought the boat was lost, that all the hard work of getting it over from America and finally clearing it out of port had gone for nothing. We feared another *Fede* affair.

The illegal boat *Fede* had been caught under similar circumstances in the harbor of La Spezia. It had taken several weeks of agitation and a hunger strike by Jewish leaders in Palestine before the British military authorities in Italy had finally permitted the boat's release.

But most of all I was afraid that the *Chalutzim* would make a desperate rush for the boat and that the police might begin shooting.

With Mrs. A——— as interpreter I went over to the leader of the *carabinieri,* pulled out my most impressive reporter's card, a red State Department card with a gold American eagle on it, and said:

"I want your name and rank."

This unexpected request took him by surprise. He asked why I wanted his name. I had a flashlight with me which I turned on the card.

Through Mrs. A———, I said:

"I'm an American newspaper correspondent here to cover the sailing of this ship and I want your name and rank because I'm going to cable to America a full description of what you and your men do on this beach tonight."

I began to hand out Camels, and the *carabinieri* were visibly softened. In the meantime, the girls among the *Chalutzim* were beginning to board the boat. I worried about them; the gangplank was so unsteady some of them might have fallen into the water.

The officer declined to give his name. I tried a new line.

"Why not let these people go?" I asked. "They'll get away eventually, as the people on the *Fede* did. You'll just have a lot of trouble for a couple of weeks and give Italy a black eye in the American press. Let the British worry about it. Why should you?"

"I can't make a decision on so important a matter," the officer of *carabinieri* replied. "I'll have to take you down to the prefecture."

Giacomo had withdrawn to a safe distance while this was going on. But when the police officer took me off, Mrs. A——— and Phil followed. I left my bags on the beach. The *Chalutzim* were still going aboard; the *carabinieri* looked on helplessly, undecided about what to do. They were afraid the prefect might decide to release the boat and they didn't know whether to stop the people from going aboard or not.

From the rear window I saw that another car had pulled away from the beach and was following us. It was Giacomo and the underground worker. They wanted to see what would happen to us and whether we would succeed in persuading the prefect to let the boat go.

IV

The sky was just beginning to show the first faint hint of dawn when we got to town. The prefecture was in what appeared to have been a *palazzo* with a big inner court-yard and an imposing broad staircase at the entrance within the court. The police station was on our right.

The officer and the sergeant on duty conversed in whispers, but we were not booked. Instead we were taken to the second floor of the building where we were ushered into a big office to wait for the prefect.

It was almost six and fully light when he arrived. He was a big, stout Italian who listened courteously while I explained that I was an American newspaper correspond-ent and made a plea for the release of the *Josiah Wedge-wood*.

He was friendly but he seemed interested in making an impression on persons more important to his future than a stray American journalist. He picked up the phone and began to speak rapidly in Italian.

Phil leaned over to me and whispered angrily:

"He's a two-faced so-and-so. He's talking to British military headquarters at Genoa and boasting that he just captured an illegal Jewish ship about to leave for Pales-tine."

"Tell him," I said to the interpreter, "that I want his

name and I'm going to telephone my paper in America immediately with the story of what he's doing."

I picked up the telephone to call a friend in Paris and ask him to call the *PM* office in New York. But the prefect took the phone away from me and said I could make no calls until after the district commissioner arrived for a hearing.

I wanted to get out of that prefecture and back to the boat somehow. I was afraid it would leave without me. I told the prefect that my earphone battery was dead and that I refused to be held for a hearing since I couldn't hear well enough to defend myself.

I said I had other batteries in my bag down on the beach and insisted that I be allowed to go back there and get them. I thought that if I could reach the beach I might be able to elude the police and go aboard.

"I don't see what difference it makes," the prefect said in Italian, "since you don't understand Italian anyway and can hear your translator well enough."

"It does matter," I insisted. "It may be that the district commissioner speaks French and that I will be able to talk directly with him."

The prefect didn't know what to do. He talked to the officer of *carabinieri*.

"They're afraid you might try to escape," Mrs. A——— explained.

Phil winked at me and said to the prefect:

"Suppose you let me go down to the beach and get Mr. Stone's bags."

The prefect agreed. Phil asked for a police pass in case, as we suspected, all the roads were being watched.

"I went downstairs," Phil told me later. "The courtyard was full of *carabinieri* who tried to stop me until I showed my pass. Outside the prefecture I saw an underground worker. He wanted to know what had happened and said he had tried to get to the boat but had been stopped and turned back by police. I told him I had a pass and jumped in his car. I told the police who stopped us on the outskirts of town that the prefect had sent me out to the beach to get the American journalist's bags.

"At the beach I found that the second convoy of trucks had arrived about three and a half hours late. They had had engine trouble twice on the way and the whole convoy waited for repairs. All but two *Chalutzim*, who were on the beach standing guard at the gangplank, had boarded the boat. Four obviously unhappy *carabinieri* talked among themselves nearby. The *Chalutzim* said everyone had got aboard safely and that the second convoy of trucks had escaped before the police could make up their minds about what to do with them.

"At this point, the *carabinieri* walked over to hear what was going on.

"I told one of the *Chalutzim* to pick up your bags and carry them to the car. On the way the underground worker told him in Hebrew that he was to give the captain his orders. He was to tell the captain to drop the gangplank as soon as possible, cut the ropes, and if necessary abandon his anchor and make a run for the open sea. 'If they start shooting,' he said, 'don't pay any attention to them but keep right on going'."

From far up the road he looked back. The boat was still there, tied tightly to the shore.

V

I got tired of waiting at the police station. While the prefect was out of the office Mrs. A———and I walked out, down the stairs, and out of the courtyard full of gendarmes. They looked surprised but didn't try to stop us.

We put in a telephone call at a hotel about five blocks away. While Mrs. A——— waited I went to a sidewalk café which was just opening and ordered coffee.

A plainclothesman and two gendarmes came over, looking very ill at ease. I invited them to join me for coffee, which they did with pleasure. When Mrs. A———arrived they explained that they wanted me to go back to the prefecture with them. I said I wanted to go back anyway, but not until I had had a second cup of coffee. When I finished, we all walked out together.

Phil had already returned to the prefecture. He told me that when he arrived he found the place in great excitement. The prefect told him I had escaped, and Phil heard him giving orders on the telephone to have all roads watched for me and to have me arrested on sight and brought back.

"You'd better be careful," Phil warned the police. "You've heard of Truman, haven't you?"

The prefect said that of course he had heard of the great American president.

"Well, Stone's a famous Washington correspondent. He is a good friend of Truman's and you'd better be careful that nothing happens to him. You may find yourself in a lot of trouble with the American government."

"There followed," Phil continued, "an excited series of rapid-fire telephone conversations in Italian in which Truman (pronounced Tru-mon, with the accent on the last syllable) was repeated many times. The police were instructed to handle you carefully and to try to bring you back without placing you under arrest."

We were less concerned about my brush with the law than with the fate of the ship and its human cargo.

The gendarmes in the courtyard made way for us when we got back. The district commissioner, a short thin Italian with pince-nez that gave him an intellectual air, was waiting for us.

Phil had my bags in the prefect's office. I took a fresh earphone battery out of one of them, first rummaging around the bag and taking out my war correspondent's jacket. This I hung carelessly over the bag, with the gold United States insignia topside so the Italians could see it.

The commissioner looked at my American passport, in which I had an Italian visa. I handed him my army travel orders as a military correspondent and insisted that I wanted to put a call through to the American Embassy in Rome. He told the prefect to place the call. We had quite a chat with the commissioner about the Jewish problem in Europe and about Palestine.

"Take the case of Tel Aviv," said the commissioner, anxious to impress us with his knowledge. "A few years ago it was only a small town. Now it's a great city."

"Why," I said to Mrs. A——— admiringly, "the commissioner knows a lot about Palestine."

The commissioner was pleased.

The officer of the *carabinieri* ran into the room. The boat had gotten away, he announced.

I pretended to be furious.

"This will ruin me professionally," I shouted. "I was supposed to be on that boat. I came all the way from America to make this trip and now you've made me miss the boat. How could a boat get away from armed police on the shore? The least you can do is to get a police launch which can overtake the boat and put me on it."

"The police were helpless," the officer said. "The men on board cut the ropes and dropped the gangplank and started off before they could do anything about it. They're out beyond territorial waters now and it would be impossible to catch them."

Just then the phone rang. My call had come through. But instead of calling the American Embassy in Rome the prefect had telephoned the British military at Genoa.

I told the British major on the phone that I didn't want to talk with him, that I wanted the American Embassy, not the British military.

"You're no American," he replied. "You're a South African. I can tell by your accent."

"Then you're a helluva judge of accents," I said.

"Let me talk to the prefect," he said.

The prefect informed me the British officer had said I was a South African and a British subject, and that I was to be held for questioning by British military authorities who were already on their way from Genoa in connection with the sailing of the illegal boat.

When I heard this I insisted on going into the next room and putting on my military correspondent's uniform. I had two reasons for this. One was to help prove to the Italians that I was an American and not a British subject. The other was to hide my notes. I didn't want them to fall into British hands.

First of all I changed into army socks. I placed my notes inside these socks.

I had hardly finished changing my socks when the colonel, the officer of *carabinieri,* the prefect and a gendarme came in to watch me dress—I suppose to make sure that I wasn't hiding anything. The colonel was very much impressed with my new green officer's uniform.

In the commissioner's office I insisted that I was an American citizen and would not wait for the British military. They called the British at Genoa again. The commissioner argued something in Italian.

All I could catch was *Tutti documenti,* meaning that I had all the necessary documents to prove my identity.

"Here, they want to talk to you," the commissioner said, handing me the telephone.

A British major who explained that he used to be a

newspaperman himself asked me if I'd wait to be questioned about the sailing.

I was pretty angry by that time. I told the British officer in not very polite language that if he used to be a newspaperman himself he ought to know this was a confidential assignment and that I wouldn't tell the British a thing.

"I'm working for my paper, not British Intelligence," I shouted. "These blankety blank police have made me miss the boat. If you want to take the responsibility of ordering my arrest, go ahead and try it. I'm walking out."

I slammed the receiver.

"I don't object to being questioned by Italian police in Italy," I said to the Italians, "but I'll be damned if I'll wait to be questioned by the British. They seem to think they're running this country."

This remark went over big with the Italians.

The commissioner said I could go if I would sign a statement saying that I knew the boat was leaving.

I wrote that I not only knew the boat was leaving but that I had been sent from America to sail on it and had missed the boat because I was illegally detained by the Italian police.

The phrase "illegally detained" seemed to worry them. They argued that I had not been arrested but had twice come voluntarily to the prefecture.

I scratched out the word "illegally" and added a post script saying that I had been very courteously treated by the Italian authorities. They were all smiles when that was translated.

They made no effort to stop us when I said, "Let's get the hell out of here."

Outside I said good-by to Mrs. A——— and Phil, jumped into a waiting car and started around the town, asking everybody we saw which was the best route to Y———. This was to give the British a false lead in the event of pursuit. I drove about ten miles out of town on the way to Y———, then took a side road in the opposite direction and late that night reached the safety of a *Haganah* headquarters.

VI

I was discouraged. There I was in an underground hideaway. It looked as though I never would succeed in making the underground trip to Palestine.

The chief underground *Haganah* emissary from Palestine in that area took a liking to me and wanted me to stay on a while with him. He was an adventurous intellectual whose escapades, when they can be told, will rival anything in Dumas. He had been assigned to underground work at the beginning of the Hitler period and had spent most of his time since then in Europe, under several dozen aliases.

I will call him Jake. He had arrived in Europe while the war was still on, and he had played his part in Allied military operations as well as in Jewish rescue work. Jake had made some amazing friends in high as well as low places.

His daring and resourcefulness, his untiring energy and the atmosphere of darkly romantic conspiracy which hung about him, appealed to his Partisan comrades. They were devoted to him. One of them said to me, "Jake's a Jewish Garibaldi."

Like many romantics, Jake regarded himself as an utter realist. He was, in fact, an extraordinarily effective person. He seemed to need little sleep and at two in the morning, when the pressure of his busy day had eased, he would drag his exhausted collaborators (and your very sleepy correspondent) to some dive for coffee, brandy, and talk. And how he could talk! He had been everywhere and read everything.

Jake had all the qualities of leadership. He could make people work outrageous hours and love it. People were proud to work with him. A love of adventure and a deep concern about human suffering were the motive springs of his character.

I was afraid that if I didn't get away soon Jake would make me forget my deadlines and go to work for him. He did his best to discourage me about the possibility of making a quick trip to Palestine. The sister ship of the boat I had helped to save was waiting in another port, but he assured me it might be weeks before it left.

"That other ship," Jake said, "is bogged down by unexpected difficulties at a very high level, as you fellows say in Washington. You might as well stay here for a while. I'm going out on a job that will make fascinating copy some day. Why don't you come along?"

The job Jake had in mind was risky, fantastic and as melodramatic as a dime novel, but if successful would be of tremendous value in further European rescue work. I suspect he succeeded. Jake's not the kind of man who permits himself to fail.

"It sounds like a wonderful story, Jake," I said, "but I'm heading back. You may be right about that other ship, but if it doesn't leave in a week I've got to fly back to America and confess that I've failed. I hate like the devil to think of walking into my office after all these weeks and telling my managing editor that I didn't get to Palestine. Maybe I'll have a lucky break yet. The whole thing might clear up. I've got to be there if that boat sails."

Jake supplied me with a car. I left at six o'clock the next morning and caught a train at the border.

UNDERGROUND TO PALESTINE

I Cross The Mediterranean

I Cross the Mediterranean

I

I reached the port in which the other ship was waiting at 10:30 that night. I checked in at a hotel and immediately went out to the boat.

I was relieved to see that it was still there, but the decks were dark and deserted. The only sound was the soft lapping of the waves against its side. I went up the gangplank to the dimly lit deck. Half the crew was celebrating in the mess.

"Izzy," they shouted, pounding me on the back, "you lucky blankety blank blank son of a blank, you're back just in time. We're sailing in the morning. Word just came that everything's cleared up. How about helping to

145

round up some of the fellows who are out making a night of it? Tell them to be sure and get back to the boat early."

I made the round of the local dives with the news. The bartenders must have thought it was some kind of V-Day. The boys had been waiting two months for this occasion.

I went back to my hotel at two in the morning, after far too many rounds of drinks. But I couldn't sleep. I fretted lest some last-minute mishap might force this ship, too, to leave without me. I finally dressed, packed my bags, woke the sleeping night clerk, paid my bill, and returned to the ship. A noisy party was still in progress, but I went to sleep in my old bunk in the officers' cabin.

I awoke early and went on deck. The sky was gray and cloudy and there was a steady drizzle. An oil barge came alongside at nine, and while we were still taking oil a lighter began to fill our water tanks. Everybody was tense and worried about the possibility that our sailing might again be postponed.

The captain was in one of his rare bad tempers. The first engineer had not shown up; two crew members were sent out to look for him.

We were to clear the harbor and pick up our passengers a half day's sail away. The two crew members sent out as a searching party were instructed to meet us there the next morning, with or without the missing engineer.

A bakery truck drove up with a load of fresh loaves of bread. Shortly before noon a second truck arrived with a company of German prisoners of war who unloaded eight crates of lifebelts and carried them up to the deck. I never did find out how German prisoners of war came

:o be loading lifebelts on an illegal boat for Jewish refugees. I thought it more discreet not to ask.

At five minutes of one the steam whistle blew and an agile crew member who used to be a Ranger in the U. S. Army climbed out on the ropes in the rain and cut away the round metal rat guards.

The compass adjusters came on board and were followed by the port pilot and his assistant. They saw crew members unpacking the lifebelts and throwing the crates on shore. The pilot smiled but made no comment. Obviously there was something odd about a big naval vessel with two dozen men in its crew which took on eight crates of lifebelts, enough for a small passenger liner.

The compass adjusters went ashore after half an hour. The pilot went up on the bridge. Crew members undid the ropes holding us to the wharf and threw them on board. We lifted our anchor. The boat began to roll gently. A tug boat came alongside. As we moved out of the harbor, the skies grew darker and a stormy north wind began to blow. We dropped the pilot and headed into rough seas.

We had a tough time of it that afternoon. The ship pitched and rolled. High dark green waves broke across our decks. I hung on to the rail on the forward deck having a wonderful time at first. I tried not to look at shipmates throwing up their lunch nearby. Soon I too began to have a strange feeling and managed to make my way to the officers' cabin and into my bunk, where I shut my eyes and tried to sleep.

I was sick, as were half the crew. I didn't get out of that

bunk until nightfall. It was my first and only bout of sea
sickness on the trip.

When I came up on deck again I found we wer
anchored about a mile offshore. The north wind was sti
blowing and a heavy rain was falling. I had on a raincoa
I had taken from the slop chest and one of those bi
sailor rainhats that tie under the chin, the kind you se
in the illustrations on Scott's emulsion.

The air was good.

We could see nothing ashore but the dark shape of
high mountain. At its foot were the few twinkling light
of a small village. There, if nothing went wrong, we wer
to pick up our passengers in the morning.

II

The boat was manned almost entirely by Americar
Jews. Most of them were American born, and at least one
—a young fellow from Arizona—was a third generatior
American. But several of them had been born in those
regions of Eastern Europe from which many of our passengers were fleeing, and one of them was a fugitive from
Hitlerism.

Many of the crew members were New Yorkers. Others
came from Chicago, Los Angeles, Baltimore, Washington, Boston, Jersey City, and New Haven. There was a

nadian boy from Toronto. Only our chief engineer was
n-Jewish.

Most of the crew had served in the Army, Navy, or
erchant Marine during the war. Some joined the crew
cause they were Zionists. A lot of them were American
halutzim who intended to remain in the collective settle-
ents in Palestine.

The rest were simply American sailors who happened
be Jews, boys with little if any past contact with Jew-
h life. They spoke neither Yiddish nor Hebrew. They
ere not very articulate, but for them the trip was more
an a heroic adventure. They all felt deeply about the
eatment of the Jews in Europe and this was their way
doing something about it.

The captain was an East European in his thirties who
d spent his life in the English, American, and Scan-
navian merchant marines. He had been born in a small
land town and just what attracted him to the sea is a
ystery even he could not explain. He began as a mess-
y. He served as first mate on two American boats which
rried war supplies for the Soviet Union to Murmansk.
e had been torpedoed. The ship on which he was first
ate was sunk in the Baltic by a German submarine. The
eboat in which he was picked up was also sunk.

The first mate was a Bronx boy who had run away
om home when he was sixteen to go to sea. He was in
e Merchant Marine during the war. He was on a liberty
ip on the Russian route in 1943 which split on the way
ck, but managed to get into English waters after three
ys of drifting with a flooded engine room. Again, on the

India route, he was on a torpedoed boat and spent a wee
in a lifeboat before he was picked up.

The second mate, whom I shall call Tom, was the so
of an Austrian-born grocer in a mid-western state. H
too, had been in the Merchant Marine during the war an
had risen from able-bodied seaman to third officer. He ha
also been in the Normany invasion. When I asked hi
what happened to him in the Normandy invasion, he sai
"Aw, nothing," and then added reflectively, "they seeme
to miss me."

Tom was one of the most interesting boys in the cre
Tall, thin, in his early twenties, he spoke neither Yiddi
nor Hebrew. I used to call him a Palestinian Popeye an
a *Lamedvovnik*.

Lamedvov means "thirty-six." A *Lamedvovnik* is "on
of the Thirty-Six." There is a Jewish legend which sa
God is dissatisfied with mankind because of its cruelt
sinfulness and greed. The reason he doesn't destroy t
world and start all over again is because there are thirt
six saints. Nobody knows who these saints are. The
saintliness is not at all obvious. Some are Jews. Some a
Gentiles. They may be white or black. They may t
learned or ignorant men. They are not necessarily pio
in an ordinary sense. One may meet a *Lamedvovnik* amor
the lowliest folk.

The *Lamedvovnik* himself is quite unconscious of bein
a saint. But these thirty-six, scattered about the world, a
people of such genuine, unaffected, and natural goodne
of heart that God finds it worth while to let an otherwi
wicked world go on for their sake.

On my trip I met a number of people I like to think of *Lamedvovnik*. One was the little British major at the P camp in Furth outside Nuremberg. The two Czech ws at Anton, the old peasant woman who gave us water we marched through her village on our way across the ustrian border, Giacomo and several of the *Haganah* nderground workers in Europe, all seemed *Lamedvov-ks*. Tom was another.

Tom was an experienced seaman, respected and readily eyed by our very independent crew. On the bridge he as a full-grown man. Otherwise he was still very much big kid. He had the sailor's distrust of people who lived 1 land; they and their tangled affairs bewildered him. Ie was always glad to get back to sea after a riotous turn 1 shore.

The chief engineer was a Scandinavian who had been sea for ten years. He was in France when France fell nd manned a refugee ship which took fleeing English-en and Frenchmen from Bordeaux to Southampton. Dur-1e occupation he lived in Denmark as a mechanic.

In 1944 he took Danish-Jewish refugees back to weden in small fishing boats and was unable to get back. Ie told me intended to send for his wife and to settle in alestine, where he hoped to become a farm machinery xpert. He was learning Hebrew, and said that life was ard in Denmark and he thought he could do better in a ew country.

One of the crew members had been a B-29 pilot. Our anadian served in the Canadian Navy during the war.)ne of our able-bodied seamen had been with the U. S.

Army Air Corps in the African and Italian campaigns.
fireman had served with the U. S. Navy's Twelfth Ar
phibious Fleet in European waters and had given up
one-third interest in a $100,000 business to go to wo.
for the illegal immigration. The second cook had been
the Army Air Force. The radio operator served as a Na
radar technician. One oiler had been in the medical bran
of the U. S. Army with the Eleventh Armored Divisic
and was with that division when its troops were throw
as reinforcements into the Battle of the Bulge.

Our German-born refugee had come to the Unite
States as a refugee in 1936. He enlisted in the Arm
served with the armored forces of the First Infantry ar
later with the Rangers. He was one of the few who su
vived Anzio Beachhead. His shipmates were proud of hir
but it was hard to get him to talk about his experience
He spoke of his many missions behind the German lin
laconically: "Aw, it was just routine work, you don't war
to hear about that." But his shipmates told me that l
once lured twelve Germans over the American lines l
pretending to be a Wehrmacht officer in the darkness.

The Ranger, as we called him, did tell me about on
of his experiences which he didn't consider routine.

His outfit was destroyed during the Anzio landin
After his escape from Anzio a soldier walked up to hi
and asked what outfit he was in. He said, "I'm a Ranger

"This other soldier took a look at me," he went on
"and asked, 'What's your religion?' I said, 'I'm a Jew.'

"He said, 'How come a Jew got into the Rangers?'

"I was so mad I pulled out my revolver and would hav

hot him, but my buddies interfered and held my arms, and my lieutenant walked up and knocked him out with a sock on the jaw."

III

The day we were to take on our human cargo for Palestine dawned raw and windy. It was drizzling when the pilot came aboard to guide us into the port at six o'clock. Our arrival didn't arouse much curiosity; we moored alongside a battered freight terminal.

While we waited for our passengers to arrive, final preparations were made to receive them. Our boat normally carried a crew of twenty-five. By building rough, unpainted wooden bunks four and five deep in every possible bit of space below decks, and in a canvas covered false deck over the stern, we had provided cramped but adequate sleeping space for more than a thousand people. There were exactly twelve hundred and forty-seven bunks on the boat and the captain told me that if he wanted to use the forepeak locker we could accommodate as many as thirteen hundred passengers.

In a special storeroom below deck we had a huge cache of canned goods, powdered eggs and other foods, including the truckload of fresh bread we had taken on the day before. We had flour and an oven in which we expected to bake bread on the voyage with the help of experienced bakers among the refugees. In a room off the galley two huge brass kettles had been set up for the stews and thick soups which were to be the main feature of meals on board. One kettle was for the orthodox Jews who wanted only kosher food. The other kettle was for the rest of us.

Amidships on deck were special canvas covered latrines and washrooms.

A few minutes after eight one of the crew members watching on deck shouted "Here they come." We saw a line of ten trucks heading for the freight terminal. They were open trucks jammed tight with refugees. As soon as the trucks stopped in the terminal the refugees began to jump off and to unload their baggage. They helped each other strap their bags and knapsacks on their backs and then shepherded by *shomrim* (guards) of their own they began to line up in regular ranks inside the big terminal shed.

There was a cold wind blowing, but one could never have guessed it from the expressions on the faces in the freight terminal. Crew members waved from the deck and shouted, *Sholom.*

Every section of the ship in which there was emergency sleeping space had been given a letter of the alphabet, and every bunk a number. One member of the crew was assigned to each section and instructed to act as usher for the refugees.

On the pier each refugee was given a slip of paper with the letter of his section and the number of his bunk. This was to speed up the loading and avoid confusion. When all those waiting had been handed their slips, a signal was given to begin the embarkation.

This was the great moment for which we had all been waiting. A group of former Partisans was given the honor of being the first to come aboard the boat. I stood at the top of the gangplank on deck to lend a hand on the final steps up, because the ascent was high and shaky.

The second mate, Tom, stood down below on the deck, took the bags from the backs of the girls and threw the bags to me so the girls wouldn't have to walk up the plank burdened. The embarkation was very orderly. Groups came on board about twenty at a time so they could be taken to their bunks before a new group boarded. The first refugee to step on deck was a husky dark-haired young Partisan from Lwow named David Pickman.

There were police all over the pier and the boat. All day long we fed them in relays in the mess. They ate as if they hadn't had enough to eat in months; the local police and port officials must have consumed several weeks' provisions that morning and drunk half a case of very fine brandy which had been saved for just such an occasion. The more they ate and drank the friendlier the atmosphere became.

Below deck, the older refugees crept wearily into their bunks while the younger ones stood in the narrow aisles chatting happily among themselves in Yiddish. One group after another came on deck in a steady stream. In the freight shed hundreds waited in orderly ranks, and from time to time new trucks rumbled into the terminal.

The people coming aboard had been traveling all night

from distant camps and cities, some more than a hundred miles away. The women looked awkward, chapped and windblown after standing ten hours in an open truck, driving over rough roads in a cold, fierce, rain.

All the passengers had a tin cup and pot hanging from the rolled blanket in which they carried their belongings. There were names or initials on most of the bags and knapsacks. One woman was carrying her baggage in a burlap bag stamped "National Sugar Refining Company, New York."

The embarkation was complicated by the fact that it had to take place on a Saturday morning, and many of the passengers were orthodox Jews. One of the underground workers said there had been considerable discussion as to whether it was permissible for such a purpose to travel and to carry bags on the Sabbath, which begins at sundown Friday evening.

The majority decided that it was *Mitzvah* (a pious deed) for a Jew to go to Palestine and that they would therefore be forgiven for what would ordinarily be a sin. But two members of the *Agudath Israel* stayed behind. They felt that even for such a purpose it was not proper to violate the Sabbath and that they would rather take their chances and wait for another ship.

Each group of trucks from a different camp or city had an underground worker as an escort. One of them described the loading.

"Imagine a dark night and a lonesome corner of a small town," he related. "The dirty little streets are unlighted. One sees no living soul as one drives into the town. Our

hree big trucks turn into a courtyard. I follow in a small
ar. In the courtyard one sees nothing, hears nothing.

"But when I get out of my car I see a long line of people,
ike shadows along the wall. They stand in silence, their
paggage already on their backs, their backs bowed. It is a
ew minutes past one in the morning, and at a signal
rom a man at the head of the line the people begin to
climb on the trucks one by one, like soldiers on the eve
of an invasion.

"I stand by the trucks and watch a group of women
and children climb on the trucks, children without
mothers, mothers without children. I look on and see
heure yunge yiddische paenemer (dear young Jewish
aces). There are packs on their backs and a hot fire in
heir eyes. Some smile. Others cry with joy. Some hug and
kiss each other and hold hands. Nobody says a word. I
ask a small girl near me—it is a cold night, with rain and
a chilling wind—'Are you cold?' She answers in a whisper,
How can I be cold on a night like this?' "

As the ship filled up, the atmosphere became hilarious.
Some of the younger children were exploring the ship,
clambering all over the place, as excited as any group of
youngsters on shipboard for the first time.

The older orthodox men began promenading the deck
for a *spazier* (promenade) in black vests and *yarmelkas*
(skull caps). In the galley, hefty volunteers from among
he refugees had set to work with housewifely zest.

Our passengers wore clothes which might have been
he leavings of several dozen secondhand shops on De-
ancey Street. The men wore everything from baggy

knickers to overalls. Many of the women had peasant kerchiefs over their heads.

The last to come aboard was Victor Baumgard, a stocky twenty-nine-year old Belgian from Arras. It had taken almost six hours to load our passengers. There were a thousand and fifteen in all. I stood at the head of the gangplank and helped every one of them aboard.

Finally the moment came when we cast off the ropes and waved good-by to the *Haganah* workers on shore.

All the refugees were ordered below decks as we prepared to make for the open sea. We did not want to arouse the curiosity of too many people on other boats and on shore. A pilot boat came alongside and slowly took us out to sea. A few minutes before six we dropped the pilot and headed south in the driving wind and rain.

Down below, the people were packed in like the cargo of an African slaver. At six-thirty, when we could see nothing but the highest mountains on the horizon and there were no other boats in sight, the captain blew a whistle as signal that the people could come up from below. The *shomrim* (guards) spread the news and our passengers streamed out on deck to look with wonder on that great sea. For them it was the sea which washes the shores of *Eretz,* whither they were bound.

IV

Among our refugees were five Gentiles who intended to settle in Palestine, four for religious, one for idealistic reasons.

Two-thirds of the refugees were men, for more men than women survived the Nazi terror. Most of our passengers were thirty years of age or younger. Only a hundred and ninety-six were over thirty. There were a few couples who had married in DP camps since the liberation. Except for the Polish Jews who had lived in the Soviet Union during the war and brought out their families under the Russo-Polish repatriation agreement, the refugees were all remnants of families.

Our oldest passenger was seventy-eight; our youngest, ten. The seventy-eight-year-old was a tall Russian *subbotnik,* a kind of Russian Seventh Day Adventist. He and his family had been converted to Judaism. He wore a black skull cap. His long head, grave eyes, and bearded face reminded one of the pictures of Anatole France in his old age. He was traveling with his wife, their son and Gentile-Polish daughter-in-law.

The son spoke fluent Yiddish as well as Hebrew. He was a *Chassid,* and with his sparse, sandy beard and flowing ear locks looked like a typical member of that pietistic Jewish sect. He said that his two brothers, who also intended to settle in Palestine, were studying at a Jewish theological seminary which had been established since the liberation in Frankfurt. One brother intended to become a rabbi, the other a *shochet,* an orthodox slaughterer.

Our other non-Jewish passenger was a twenty-four-year-old French girl from Grenoble, a shy, slight, quiet person. Her father was a gentleman farmer. During the war she worked in the French resistance. There she first met Jews in helping some of them escape deportation to Germany. She got to know several of the Jewish resistance leaders and became interested in Zionism. When I asked her why she was going to Palestine, she said she felt that she could best lead a truly socialist life by entering one of the Jewish collective settlements in the Holy Land.

Our ten-year-old was a dark-haired Polish-Jewish girl named Judith Greenberg. She was clever, sharp-tongued, and precocious, and wrote poetry in Polish. After her parents had been sent to their deaths at Treblinka, her aunt had escaped with her from the Warsaw ghetto and, giving her the name of Szofel, had placed her in a Polish orphan home as a Christian child. The aunt had lived with false Aryan papers as a Polish slave laborer in Germany, and had come back for her after the liberation.

"That child," the woman told me proudly, "has crossed five borders illegally on her way to this ship."

With them was the woman's husband, a broad-shouldered man of medium height who had been in the Polish Army in 1939, in a Russian camp as a prisoner of war, and in the Polish Army again until the end of the war.

There were Jews from sixteen different countries on board, including one rather lonely Egyptian Jew who spoke only his native Arabic and a smattering of French. He had gone to Italy as a laborer before the war and been deported to a German concentration camp as a "non-Aryan."

There were five hundred and eighty-five refugees from Poland. The next largest national group, a hundred and nine, were Czechoslovakian Jews, most of them from Slovakia and Carpatho-Russia. There were eighty-four immigrants from Holland, all young people. Some of them were German and Austrian Jews who had gone to Holland before the war to escape Nazi persecution. But many were Dutch, members of families which had settled in Holland in the sixteenth century after the exodus from Spain.

The Dutch youngsters looked like illustrations from *Hans Brinker and the Silver Skates*. Their parents had been deported to Germany and killed by the Nazis. They were not fleeing Holland—they were going to Palestine. They spoke of their native land with sad affection, but they were *Chalutzim*, Zionist pioneers bent on building a Jewish homeland. English rather than Yiddish was their secondary language.

One of them, a plump, rosy girl of twenty-two, expressed the nationalist awakening which was sending these youngsters to a new and difficult country in a kind of fierce, proud reaction to the events of the Hitler period. She too had lost her parents to the Germans.

"I never was a Jew before the war. But now that six million Jews have been killed, I will be a Jew too," she said with an air of cheerfully stubborn defiance.

There was a lovely girl in the group from Holland, a

tall, graceful Viennese named Ilse Walter. She was twenty-six and had intended to be a chemist. She had fled to Holland under false papers when the Nazis occupied Austria and had remained there throughout the occupation. Part of the time she lived in hiding in the home of the present Dutch Minister of Agriculture. He was an underground leader and sheltered many fugitives, including political prisoners, escaped prisoners of war, Jews, and British Intelligence agents. Later she worked as a nurse in an Old Peoples' Home in Amsterdam, where only the Dutch director know she was Jewish. So far as she knew, her whole family had been killed except for an uncle, who before the war had settled in Palestine, and possibly her father, who had escaped from a German concentration camp into Russia before the Nazi attack on the Soviet Union.

There were fifty-nine Jews from Hungary, fifty-one from Rumania, forty-four from Germany. Twenty-four were from Lithuania. Twenty were from France, twelve from Belgium, and eleven from Austria. There were six Russian Jews, three Latvians, two Swiss, two Turkish, two Greek, and the Egyptian. One of the Latvian Jews had settled in Palestine before the war and gone back to Riga in 1939 to see his parents. He had been there when the war began.

Linguistically, the ship was a floating Babel. Yiddish varies considerably from country to country and there were about a dozen different dialects aboard. Even from those countries in which Yiddish was the common language of the Jews, there were many who had been completely

ssimilated and spoke only the native language of their
irthplaces.

The two Turks spoke *Ladino,* the Mediterranean and
Levantine counterpart of Yiddish spoken by descendants
of Spanish Jews scattered by the Inquisition. It is mixed
Spanish and Hebrew, as Yiddish is basically mixed German and Hebrew. The Greeks, a man and his wife who
married in Paris after the liberation, spoke only Greek
and French. The husband was the tallest man on board,
a man who might have served as a model for Praxiteles.
He was deported from Greece to a German concentration
camp in 1942. Everyone was curious to know his occupation. When I asked him he said he was a pastry cook.

One hundred and thirty-eight persons on board had no
party affiliation. The rest belonged to seventeen different
Zionist parties, the largest group being orthodox. There
were one hundred and ninety-five members of *Agudath
Israel* and ninety of *Poale Mizrachi* (orthodox labor).
Next were a hundred and forty revisionists, chauvinistic
and right wing. There were eighty-two *Chalutzim* from
the *Hashomer Hatzair,* a left-wing socialist group which
advocates a bi-nationalist Arab-Jewish Palestine rather
than a Jewish state.

Of the thousand and fifteen passengers, five hundred
and sixty-eight were *Chalutzim* who intended to spend
their lives in collective settlements in Palestine. All of
them were socialists of one kind or another.

V

More than three hundred of the refugees had served during the war in the Red Army, the Polish Army, the Czech Army, or with the Partisans.

The youngest of these war veterans was a boy of thirteen. His name was Hersh Arbas and he came from Warsaw. He was a cute little fellow and allowed the run of the bridge as a special pet of the captain and the crew. He wanted some day to be a sailor. He was the youngest of three small boys in berets on board, all three of them as agile and noisy as monkeys. They had an uproarious time during the voyage, playing hide-and-go-seek around the decks and climbing up and down the rigging. Hersh was the envy of his two friends because he had carried a revolver and lived and fought with a group of Polish Partisans.

Hersh's father had been a wealthy man, and he had sufficient means to buy safety for several years. From 1939 to 1942 he lived hidden in a Polish farmhouse with his father, mother, and small sister. In 1942 there was a raid on the farmhouse and the Germans took his parents away. He never saw them again. Hersh and his four-year-old sister remained in hiding with the farmer, who had been paid by Hersh's father to take care of them. But one day Hersh saw police coming to the farmhouse and concluded that they had been betrayed.

"I grabbed my sister by the hand," Hersh told us, "and we ran out the back door toward a nearby forest. The police saw us and opened fire. One shot killed my sister but I got away. I hid in the woods by day and traveled by night, and managed to reach the ghetto in Krosnick. I'd only been there a few weeks when the Germans rounded up thirty of us, mostly older people, and put us on a death wagon for the crematorium.

"On the way, when it got dark, one of the older men threw me over the side of the wagon into a ditch and jumped in after me. We stayed there until the wagon was out of sight. We wandered around for twelve days. A party of German soldiers caught sight of us from a distance and opened fire, killing the man with me. A truck loaded with flour was passing at the time, and I jumped on the back of it and got away. There were nails on the road put there by Partisans to sabotage traffic. When a tire blew out and the driver stopped the truck to fix it, Partisans hiding along the road killed him.

"The Partisans were friendly. They instructed me to use a false Polish name and left me with a rich peasant. I stayed with him for eight months until he began to suspect that I was a Jew. I fled to a small town. The town was surrounded by the Germans several nights later in an effort to capture Partisans hiding out in it. There was heavy fighting in the raid. I don't know what happened to me, but I woke up to find myself with a bandaged head in a forest hideout with a group of Partisans."

Hersh remained with these Partisans until the area in

which they operated was liberated by the Russians in 1945. They gave him a Russian revolver.

"Yah!" he said with a broad smile when I asked him if he ever used it.

The Partisans were Poles, except for their captain and their doctor, who were both Russians. These two were the only ones who knew that he was Jewish. After the liberation the Partisan captain placed Hersh in a Jewish children's home run by the orthodox *Agudath Israel*.

There were experienced military men among us who had been tailors, storekeepers, weavers, locksmiths, and woodworkers in the ghettoes of Poland before the war. I talked with one who had been a locksmith in Pinsk. When the Russians occupied that part of Poland in 1939 he was drafted into the Red Army and sent to an officers' school in Leningrad where he became a tank specialist with the rank of lieutenant. He fought all through the siege of Leningrad and was later assigned to the Polish forces and participated in the liberation of Warsaw.

A carpenter from Pinsk had become a Partisan commander. His band worked in close contact with the Red Army and he was awarded a Stalin medal after the liberation.

A Jew from Lodz had had a varied career as an artillery officer. He fought in the Polish Army in 1939, was captured by the Russians when they invaded Poland and held a prisoner of war until 1941. When the Nazi invasion began he volunteered for the Red Army. He served eight months in the Russian Army and then three and a half years in the Polish Army. When the war ended he did not wait to be demobilized. He took advantage of a fourteen-day leave to escape across the Czech border. There was nothing to keep him in Poland, he said; all his relatives were dead and the Polish Army very anti-Semitic.

Some of the Jews had survived in peculiar ways. With us was a Polish Jew from Cracow who had owned a large printing establishment before the war. He was sent to Auschwitz, but soon found himself transferred on a strange assignment.

"Several other Jews and I were summoned to the camp headquarters one day," he related, "and told to make ready for a journey. We were taken to a concentration camp at Sachshausen near Berlin. Sachshausen was a camp for political prisoners. This fact was known abroad and the camp was never bombed.

"We were placed in a special underground section of the camp from which even SS men were barred. There were one hundred and forty of us there—all printers and all Jews, from France, Italy, and Czechoslovakia as well as from Poland. Except for the fact that we were kept closely confined we were well treated and well fed. We were put to work counterfeiting foreign currency and foreign documents for the Gestapo."

This man told me an incredible story. He said he had once been congratulated on his birthday by Heinrich Himmler, the head of the Gestapo.

"It was in 1944," he told me. "I was foreman on the night shift and the workers under me had planned a little celebration for my birthday. That night Himmler came to visit the counterfeiting plant. With him was the Nazi leader Kaltenbrunner. You must understand that we were a favored group, treated well and never beaten. Himmler was very pleased with the work we were turning out, and when he came in and saw some birthday decorations on the wall he asked whose birthday it was. 'Let him stand forth,' Himmler ordered. When I walked up to him and saluted, he asked: 'Who are you?'

" 'I'm a Polish Jew,' Herr Commisar,' I said.

"Himmler shook hands with me and wished me a happy birthday. He said he was pleased with the work my shift was doing and asked what I would like for my birthday. I was taken aback by his friendliness, and I still don't know how I had the courage to do it, but I pointed to a paper placard put up on the wall for the birthday party which had one word on it—*Freiheit*.

" 'Only that,' I said, my knees a little shaky.

"Himmler answered with an odd smile, *'Es kommt'* (it is coming). I don't suppose the freedom he meant was more than the 'freedom' which came to those of our comrades who fell ill and were taken away never to reappear. None of us who worked there was ever intended to know freedom again except in the other world. But freedom was coming all the same, and I was permitted to see it."

I can't vouch for this story. All I can report is that it was told me in a matter-of-fact way one morning by a man who did not seem to be lying. When I asked him what happened after that, he added a detail of a kind that made me think his story was authentic. He said Himmler ordered one of the guards to give the printer a special issue of a hundred and thirty cigarettes for his birthday. The odd,

xact number and the anti-climactic detail seemed to me
ae kind of thing one does not fabricate. I think a Mun-
hausen would have thought of a more dramatic climax.

VI

There was a man on board whom we all called Rudy
nd a girl I shall call Ruth. Theirs was the most exciting
tory I heard on my trip. In some ways it was a horrible
tory.

When I heard it I kept thinking of a famous Latin
aying whose source I have forgotten, *"Homo homini
upus."* This is usually translated "man preys on man"
)ut literally it means, "man is a wolf to man."

The story is the more dreadful because the hero, Rudy,
was himself part wolf. It was this streak of fierce and
)redatory criminality that made it possible for him to sur-
/ive and to help others to survive.

The story of Rudy and Ruth has elements of beauty as
well as horror, for it is a story of courage in the face of
:error, degradation, loneliness, and death.

I spoke of having heard this story. Actually I had to
piece it together, to draw it out bit by bit in the course of
several talks. I have added nothing to it. It is too melodramatic to need any gloss of the fictional, and this glimpse
of human beings in hell is too memorable for anything
but the truth.

Rudy was not the real name of the hero. I do not know his real name, nor would I print it if I did, for he was one of the leading figures of the underground which has been rescuing Jews from Europe since the beginning of the Hitler period. Ruth was only one of many hundreds whom he saved.

Ruth was a *chalutzah,* a pioneer in Zion, a member of the left-wing *Hashomir Hatzair* or Young Guard, a Marxist Zionist group.

Ruth was twenty. Rudy was in his fifties. I first met him on the seacoast of a European country bordering the Mediterranean. He was described as the foremost character among the refugees there, a Jew whom the others called *Shimshon Ha-Giboor,* or Samson the hero. The Hebrew is that applied to the original Samson in the Bible.

He was an ox of a man, a sort of Jewish Man Mountain Dean, with big brown eyes and a short brown beard. He had the hoarse, rasping voice of a man accustomed to shouting orders at crowds.

We did not become friends at once. Rudy shied away from me when he was told that I was an American newspaperman. There was very little that could frighten Rudy but he looked scared when I took out my notebook and pencil while talking with him.

There was always a little knot of curious admirers and hangers-on around Rudy.

He called me aside—that first day I met him ashore—and, in as close to a whisper as that bull's voice of his would allow, asked: "Are you going with us on the boat to *Eretz?"*

He eyed me shrewdly, like one not accustomed to being deceived. I was under strict orders to tell no one that I was going to travel the underground route to Palestine. I shrugged my shoulders as though the thought had never occurred to me, and said I didn't know. Rudy looked down at me for a moment, then with a satisfied grin slapped me heartily on the back.

"We'll talk on the boat," he said, "but not one word now. If a word gets out to the papers before I leave . . ." he made a quick motion with his big hand across his thick throat.

Some of the things I heard about Rudy were so incredible that I checked his story with friends in the underground. They were a sober little band, too genuinely heroic themselves for heroics and much too busy to brag. They vouched for him.

Rudy was a Polish Jew who had been orphaned at the age of eight. He was then twice as big and strong as any boy his age. He made his way to Cuba before the First World War and grew up in the streets of Havana. After the war he became a rum runner and served a term in a U. S. Federal penitentiary where he made friends with a well-known American gangster—not a man of Capone's structure but an important man in the business.

Rudy went back to rum running after his release from prison. When the repeal of prohibition ended that occupation, he became a professional wrestler, and later a strong man in a circus. He was in Europe on tour with a circus in 1939 and the war caught him in Poland.

Rudy was captured by the Nazis and sent to a concentration camp as a Jew. There his size and strength attracted attention; the Germans used him constantly, as they might a fine farm animal, for blood transfusions. I do not know all that happened to him. He said once that it would take a whole book to tell his life adequately. I know that he turned up a couple of years later in the camp at Auschwitz, notorious for its cruelty and crematoriums. It was there that the adventure of Rudy and Ruth took place.

I first met Ruth on board the boat our second night out. I was wandering around the deck, talking to as many people as I could and soaking it all in—the starry sky, the lonely Mediterranean, the happy singing, the crowds of Jews milling about on deck as they might on Delancey Street or Petticoat Lane. Then I saw a girl who looked very sick sitting on the deck with her back against the superstructure amidships. (I hope that's the proper nautical way to say it.)

I asked if I could help her, but she only smiled wanly, pointed to her stomach and said she'd be all right. She looked as though company was the last thing in the world she wanted. I went away. The next night she looked much better. I asked her how she felt and struck up a conversation.

She was a Polish Jew of a rather well-to-do family. Like most people on that boat, she had lost her family in concentration camp and crematorium. She, too, had been at Auschwitz, under sentence of death as a political prisoner.

"Have you noticed that big fellow on deck?" she asked. She did not call him Rudy but used another name, which I presume is his real one. I knew at once whom she meant. I nodded.

"I never expected to see him alive again," she said. "He saved my life at Auschwitz. I never did know what happened to him afterward until I met him again on this boat."

Ruth was not a glamour girl. In the first place she was fat, not obesely broad-beamed like so many of the women on board, but certainly plump. Perhaps the plumpness was, in part, occupational. For Ruth had been studying a practical trade which would be useful in a collective settlement in Palestine. She chose to be a dairy maid, and after years of Nazi concentration fare she loved nothing better than bread and milk. She admitted that she had indulged in this liking every few hours while working as a milkmaid, and the result was to obliterate any possible resemblance she might once have had to a pretty girl.

Secondly, Ruth never combed her hair. It was a wild, unruly mop of black curls that she brushed back with her hands, or blew back with protruding lower lip, when it got in her eyes which were blue and beautiful, or when it interfered with her conversation, which was brilliant, and—when she found somebody she liked—unending, as if to make up for years of silence.

As a pioneer woman-to-be she affected to despise feminine graces. She loved to tell how her incorrigible milkmaid manners had shocked a wealthy and sophisticated aunt in Brussels who had tried to dissuade her from going to Palestine and to make her into a leisured lady.

Her favorite costume consisted of dungarees, for which

Nature had not entirely suited her, and a leather zipper jacket, which she wore with a swagger. She never used rouge or lipstick, but her rosy cheeks and creamy skin needed neither. Despite her contempt for femininity she was something of a charmer, a bit of a flirt, and after the first few nights always had a fascinated coterie of boys from the crew and the *Chalutzim* around her. She was witty, vivacious, a born raconteur. She was no rapt-eyed listener. The boys could hardly get a word in edgewise, but they found her enchanting. So did I.

The most amazing thing about Ruth was the wholesomeness and naiveté with which she had emerged from her concentration camp experiences. She was a child, but an extraordinarily perceptive one. She was very quick to understand the essential qualities of the people she met on shipboard, as I knew from her reactions to the various members of the crew, whom I had known longer and more intimately than she had. I called her "wonder child" or "young cow," depending on how I felt about her at the moment. She was both. She was widely read and could describe her past experiences with a vividness that made me encourage her to write.

The first night we really talked we stood by the rail watching the phosphorescent glow of the waves breaking against the ship, and looking at the stars.

"You can't imagine what life was like in a concentration camp," Ruth said. She pointed to the stars. "It's as if I were to come down from one of the planets and tried to explain what life was like in another world. Even now, a year after the liberation, I find it hard to believe some of the things that happened to me and to other people. To see people around you beaten, hanged, and shot as part of what was a normal round, always to expect the same fate yourself tomorrow, that was our daily life."

That night she described her feelings the night before her scheduled execution at Auschwitz.

"I was in a bunker, a prison half underground, with a small window near the top of the wall. I stood all that night on a box, looking out at the stars. Around campfires outside, Gypsies were waiting for the wagons which would take them to the gas chambers and the crematorium. I have never seen such beautiful creatures, men and women with black eyes and the handsome swarthy faces of free wild creatures. They were very friendly to us in the camp because they shared with the Jews the brunt of the Nazi extermination campaign. They were very brave. I cried for them and for their courage, not for myself. That I was to be executed was something I could not really grasp.

"I felt my hand and said to myself, 'This is my hand,' and I felt my face and said 'This is my face,' I felt my head and said 'This is my head, and tomorrow all this that is me will exist no longer because somebody wills it so'."

But Ruth did not die that next day. Her life was spared by reason of the strange ascendancy which Rudy, a Jew, had managed to achieve in the camp.

Rudy's rise began with a hundred and twenty lashes he received the day he entered Auschwitz. He had been caught near a frontier town and was rightly suspected of working in what the Germans felt was the beginning of a Jewish underground rescue organization. He denied any such connections; the lashes were intended to make him talk. Fifty were enough to wreck an ordinary man and Rudy did gratefully lapse into unconsciousness long before he had taken the full hundred and twenty. They were administered by two men who stood on either side of him and brought their bullwhips down alternately on his naked back.

"I wouldn't give those bastards the satisfaction of hearing a Jew cry out," Rudy said, "and I bit hard on my tongue to keep silent before I passed out. It took me several weeks to recover from that beating, but I never told them what they wanted to know. The beating had one strange result. The SS camp commander saw me undergo what no ordinary person could have survived, and in his own way he took a liking to me.

"He was a tall man, very thin, and he loved cruelty. He is still alive somewhere in Germany—in fact some months ago I heard that he was trying to reach me to testify on his behalf to Allied War Crimes investigators."

I felt that Rudy rather liked the fellow.

The SS camp commander made Rudy a *kapo* and later promoted him to be chief *kapo* for one whole section of Auschwitz. The word *kapo* is German, an abbreviated form for *katzet polizei* (concentration camp police). *Kapos* were chosen from among the inmates, Jewish *kapos* from the Jews, Polish *kapos* from the Poles. Besides keeping order they did the dirty work of the Nazis, beating their own people, spying upon them, and currying favor with the Nazis at the expense of their fellows. But a few used their influence to help their own people. A few were heroes who worked with the underground under the very noses of their Nazi masters to help others escape. Rudy was one of these.

As head *kapo* Rudy was not without means, if he had the resourcefulness to use them and the nerve to risk death in doing so. For one thing there was a closely guarded storeroom at Auschwitz where the Nazis kept gold, jewelry, money, and other valuable taken from Jews who had been sent to be gassed and burned. SS men were denied access to this room. The valuables were the property of the state. The storeroom was guarded by Jews; every few months the guards would be sent to the crematorium and new ones would be assigned their places. For a Jew to be caught in the camp with valuables of this kind meant instant death. Rudy risked it.

Rudy organized a kind of black market at Auschwitz which dealt in everything, including human beings. He bribed guards with cigarettes, brandy, meat, and luxuries to establish underground connections between the various camps for rescue work. As his reputation grew, Rudy found that he had another source of funds. Those Jews who had managed to conceal some valuables up to the very doors of the gas chambers turned these over to the Jews who drove the death wagons, asking that they be handed over to Rudy. The drivers usually did so out of fear of what would happen to them if such things were found in their possession when they got back to camp.

As Rudy grew bolder he brought the SS commander under his influence.

"I had a jeweler in the camp," Rudy told me, "make
up a gold ring with two diamonds from the storehouse. I
took it to the SS commander, clicked my heels, saluted, and
said, 'Herr Oberkommandant, I found this' and handed
him the diamond ring. He looked me in the eye and said,
'What do you mean by saying you found this?' I repeated
that I had found it. He asked, 'Why didn't you take it to
the chief of your section? Why did you bring it to me?'
I kept a straight face and answered, 'I didn't think I had
to take it to him. I thought you might like to have it.' He
grabbed me by the shoulders and peered full into my face
for several minutes. But he finally took the ring. He knew
from those hundred and twenty lashes, that I was a man
who could keep my mouth shut. From that time on a new
relationship developed between us.

"He liked women and I found out that he was keeping
several in Germany. He needed money. I saw to it that he
was well supplied. Every week I would slip out a bit of
jewelry he could send to a girl friend, or smuggle out a
bit of gold for him. He began to depend on me and when
I needed a favor I could usually get it from him. All this
was very valuable for the underground. We weren't able
to do very much, but that little was precious."

One of the things he had been able to do was to save
Ruth. Ruth was caught in Vienna after leaving Poland
in 1942 with false Aryan papers. She had been asked by a
friend to carry a message. She did not know what the
message was, all she knew was that it had something to
do with an illegal organization. She asked no questions
for the less information one had the less there was to tell

under torture. She was accused of being a communist underground worker, sentenced to death by hanging, and shipped to Auschwitz for execution. I tell it quickly here, and Ruth told it quickly to me, but I gathered there were many days of questioning in Vienna and that the methods used were not pleasant to recall.

"I had never been in a concentration camp before," Ruth said. "When I got to Auschwitz I was put into a big bunker with two hundred other girls. The others were all Polish and some were very unfriendly. They found out I was a Jew and there were many gibes at my expense. I didn't expect to live, but I was determined to show them how a Jew could die.

"One of the Polish girls mocked, 'So you're a Jew, are you? Well, I guess Rudy will try to help you. He's always doing things for Jews.' I didn't know who Rudy was and when he appeared the next day I didn't like him. He said he would try to help me, but I felt that I was beyond help. I thought he was just a big talker. I was preparing myself to die bravely and I didn't want to be bothered by false hopes.

"Rudy came back the next day and brought me a pretty dress. I had nothing to wear so I put it on, and I was foolish enough to feel pleased. I didn't realize then that he got the dress by taking it from a body in the gas chamber. I didn't know yet that in a concentration camp every breath one drew was at somebody else's expense."

Rudy interrupted to tell me how he felt when he first saw Ruth.

"Ha!" Rudy said, "she was stubborn and unfriendly.

But when I first set eyes on her I loved her as if she were
my own daughter. She was such a sweet child. I couldn't
let her go to her death. I had to find some way to save her."

"I knew Ruth was supposed to be hanged the next
morning," Rudy went on. "I had very little time to lose.
I got to my friend the commander at about two in the
morning. I brought with me a bottle of the best *schnapps*
I had. The commander was a great drinker. I never met
another man with his capacity. I fed him the *schnapps* and
gave him a shave. He liked me to shave him. By the time
I was through there was a great deal of *schnapps* under
his belt and he was in a cheerful mood. He pinched my
cheek and said, 'Well, Rudy my boy, what can I do for
you?' I said, 'Herr Oberkommandant, I have a favor to ask
that means a great deal to me.' He said, 'If it's anything
within reason you shall have it.'

" 'You know that Jewish girl in the Polish bunker," I
said. He looked serious at once. I said, 'I'm in love with
that girl and I must have her. Give me her life.'

"The commander screamed at me, 'Rudy, you're crazy.
That's impossible. She's no ordinary Jew you can spirit
away. She's a traitor to the state. There's a whole carload
full of documents on her. This is too big. I can't do anything'."

Rudy played his last card. He knew how dependent the
commander had grown on the money and jewels Rudy
brought him.

"I said to him, 'Herr Oberkommandant, if that girl dies
I die too. I can't live without her. If she hangs tomorrow
I'll take my life the same day.'

"The SS commander looked at me with fury in his eyes. I looked straight back at him without dropping mine. I tried to look calm, but I didn't feel calm. I felt my knees would give way as I waited for his decision. The next few minutes were the most anxious I've ever spent.

"Finally the commander shouted at me, 'You crazy Jew, how can such a thing be done?' Then I knew I had won. I had a plan ready and while he blustered and raged I explained it to him."

There had to be a body. A death certificate had to be sent to higher authorities. The means by which a substitute body and a false certificate may be obtained are too dreadful to relate. But before dawn that morning false Aryan papers had been made out for Ruth and she was sent under special guard to a labor camp for Polish girls.

Almost the first question Ruth asked Rudy when they met on the boat was, "Whatever happened to your Czech friend?"

One day the SS brought a prisoner to Auschwitz who was a Czech army officer. He was a Jew and Rudy took an instant liking to him.

"He was a man," Rudy said with emphasis. "He had blue eyes that were afraid of nothing. He carried himself like a true soldier, and he treated his SS captors with calm contempt. I loved him," said Rudy, pounding his big fist against his heart, "and I wanted to help him get away."

Ruth told me the story as she had seen and heard it from the prison.

"I first heard about the officer from Rudy on one of his visits to me," she related. "I wasn't surprised a few days later to hear that the Czech had escaped. I was amused to learn that after the escape Rudy had stormed up and down the camp making the most bloody threats as to what he would do to that cursed Jew if he were ever recaptured. 'I'll flog him to death with my own hands!' Rudy had cried. But that night he came to me and danced up and down with joy as he told me of the escape.

"Unfortunately the Czech was recaptured about a week later. He was sentenced to be hanged. The SS authorities suspected that Rudy had had a hand in the escape and planned to punish him too. Ordinarily Jews were hanged by Poles and Poles by Jews as part of a deliberate plan to make the two peoples hate each other more. But on this occasion Rudy was ordered to hang his friend with his own hands."

"I almost went crazy," Rudy broke in. "I didn't know what to do. I went to the leaders of the Jews in the camp and asked them to advise me. They said, 'Rudy, nothing can help that man. He must die. If you try to interfere you will lose your life, too, and you are the only person here who can help us a little. The man must die and you must obey the authorities and hang him'."

Ruth recalled how that Czech Jew looked the morning set for the execution.

"I saw him go marching proudly past my bunker, his head erect. He stopped and threw me a kiss. He knew of me through Rudy, and his eyes said a beautiful farewell."

When the Czech came with his hands bound and his mouth gagged to the scaffold, he looked Rudy in the eye "as though trying to tell me not to be afraid, that he understood, that he did not blame me, that we were still good friends and to go ahead."

But Rudy had already made up his mind to risk everything rather than hang his friend.

"I always carried a razor blade hidden on me for use as a kind of last resort," he said. "Shortly before the hanging was to take place I took my razor blade and cut into both sides of that rope, just enough for my purpose. When I put the noose around his neck and pulled the lever that opened the trap door he dropped, but it was the rope that broke, not his neck. The Germans took him away to another camp. They ordered me hanged in his place. But my friend the SS commander saved me. He insisted that the fault lay with the rope and not me, and demanded that he be allowed to test a length of the same rope. But in the test he used a section of iron rail so heavy that it broke the rope. The commander claimed that this showed that I was the innocent victim and that the rope had been rotten."

I asked Rudy what happened afterwards to the Czech officer.

"I don't know," he said sadly. "I assume he was executed. I never heard from him again."

VII

The first part of our trip to Palestine took eight days. It was uneventful and happy, despite the discomforts.

The discomforts had largely to do with our sleeping arrangements. The low, narrow wooden bunks were of a kind on which only the young, healthy, and dog-tired could find rest. The few mattresses were reserved for the sick. The rest lay down in their clothes or spread blankets on the splintery, unfinished lumber.

There was little ventilation below deck and at night the air grew stale and stinking. Bare feet stuck out from the bunks into the passageways. The silence was broken by coughing, the sighs of the sleepless, and the moans of the sick. Sleepy-eyed young *shomrim* stood or sat on watch all night at the gangways below deck. The real heroes were the weary members of the sanitation squad who came running with buckets and mops whenever the seasick were too ill to go on deck. Each case would set off others unless and until there was a quick cleanup.

A corps of two dozen boys and girls with red *Mogen Dovid* armbands who had been given a course in first aid brought lemons and wet compresses for the seasick, comforted the frightened, slapped the occasional hysteric, and gave injections in a few cases of heart disease. One of the nurses was a big Hungarian girl who was stronger than most of the men on board. She was very proud of the American slang she had picked up. She had the right combination of tenderness, roughness, and strength for a good nurse. It was one of the memorable sights of the voyage to see her grab a sick man around the neck, open his mouth and force a spoonful of unpleasant medicine down his throat. With her big arms, black eyes and dark skin she looked like a young gypsy matriarch.

The seriously ill were taken to the doctor's office, a small room below deck which was normally used as the officers' mess. But on this voyage the officers ate with the crew and the mess had been fitted up with two bunks for the doctor and his wife. A big makeshift cabinet held a small crateload of medicines and instruments.

The doctor was one of our illegal immigrants. He was a slight man of middle height who had been born in Bukovina but lived in France since the first World War. His black-haired, vivacious wife was a French Jew, and their little cabin was the social center for our French colony. The French and Belgian youngsters foregathered there and the cabin was always full of French conversation and French songs. The doctor had worked with the Maquis during the war. He was an idealist. He said he did not wish to practice in the cities but to become the doctor member of one of the new collective settlements.

Of course, the news that there was a *Herr Doktor* aboard, and that his services were free, enthralled the hypochondriacs. There were always women in his cabin, crying in Yiddish, "Oh, Doctor, I'm dying . . . I'm fainting. . . . Oh, Doctor, I'll never get to Palestine."

The doctor was a cultured man and enjoyed talking about books and politics. When interrupted by one of these grave cases he was likely to shout unfeelingly:

"Nothing is going to happen to you. You're not going to die."

He would give these "sick" a couple of sugar pills or a slice of lemon, and sometimes add in an exasperated aside to me, intended for the ears of the sick one:

"What's she bothering me for? She's as healthy as a horse."

The hypochondriacs were convinced that the doctor was a monster.

After two days of stormy weather, we came into calm and sunny seas. The most determined hypochondriacs succumbed to the restful beauty of the Mediterranean, the languorous days and starry nights. Even the woman we called the Sleeping Beauty gave in to the fine weather after three days and sat up.

For four days she had lain, wrapped in a blanket on top of a life raft on the forward deck, just in front of and below the bridge. She was the most beautiful woman on board, a graceful lovely creature of twenty. Her husband, a handsome Polish engineer in his late thirties, led a miserable life putting compresses on her head, helping her when she vomited, and coaxing her to take a little food. We learned that she was four months with child.

The Sleeping Beauty and her husband had a very romantic story. They lived and worked as Aryans under the Germans. They met and fell in love. Each discovered that the other was Jewish. They had married after the liberation. She was the engineer's second wife. He had lost his first family.

Whenever we sighted another ship our passengers were quickly herded below lest our crowded decks arouse suspicion. Each time that happened, the decks were washed and swept. These periods below and the nights were the worst for our people. There was a curfew at eleven o'clock when all the passengers had to go to bed. They began to come up again before dawn.

The food was not too bad, but neither was it too plentiful. There was plenty of bread, which I thought delicious, although our four refugee bakers complained and apologized every day about the inadequate oven. The meals consisted largely of a combination stew and soup for the non-kosher and a thick vegetable soup for the kosher. There was little coffee or tea except for the crew, the nurses, and the men of the sanitary squad. Perhaps the man who suffered most from the meals was our chief cook, an American *Chalutz*, who worried constantly that he wasn't able to serve quite enough. He grew so melancholy that the crew stopped kidding him about his cooking, which had been one of our favorite occupations at mess.

Early in the morning the orthodox began to come out on deck to pray, putting on their prayer shawls and phylacteries and bowing energetically toward the east.

Breakfast was served at about seven, most people eating on deck. The passengers organized themselves into groups, and each group leader with a helper brought up the food in buckets, with paper dishes and fresh loaves of bread. Cigarettes and chocolate were given out several times during the voyage. There was powdered milk for those who needed it. Lunch was served at noon and dinner at six.

Despite the discomforts and shortcomings, there never was a gayer ship on the high seas. Our decks looked like Orchard Beach or Coney Island on a hot Sunday. They were packed with people in every possible costume, from bathing suits to the black mohair vests of the shirt-sleeved older orthodox men.

Below us one day three caps and one *yarmelka* were eating hardtack smeared with butter while they carried on a voluble conversation. A girl played a concertina on top of a pile of life rafts, surrounded by admirers. A fat red-head with a purple hair ribbon sat by herself on a hatch, happily singing a Hebrew song and rocking back and forth to the rhythm. Two lovesick calves held hands as they sat along the rail: she plump, he thin with horn-rimmed spectacles. They kissed soulfully. An unshaven little man with a red Turkish cap wandered around in search of something, looking like an organ grinder's lost monkey.

Big, fat Rudy, the ex-circus strong man, dressed only in white shorts with a towel wrapped around his head like a turban, sat on a ventilator, swarthy, fierce, and bearded as a wild Mongol chief or galley slavemaster. A group of *Chalutzim* were dancing the Palestinian *hora,* holding hands in a great moving circle as they leaped and sang.

The first mate sat on the railing of the bridge, contentedly smoking a cigar as he looked on.

"Yes," he said, as if after profound reflection, "it's the old Hudson River Day Line all over again—next stop, Bear Mountain."

VIII

So little happened during the first week of our journey that we were completely unprepared for the dangers and hardships which were to arise on our way through the blockaded waters of Palestine. Our ship could have made the entire trip in four days and our slow progress puzzled us. But since the trip was pleasant we paid scant attention to the leisurely pace. The reason for our loitering was soon to become apparent.

During that first week on board, a ship's paper would have been hard put for news. I spent my time talking with the passengers. There was hardly one aboard whose life would not have made an exciting story. That week on the Mediterranean was the first peaceful interlude they had enjoyed in years.

There was a bit of excitement the third day out when two long-lost cousins met each other on the foreward deck with shouts of joy, hugs, and kisses. The fourth day the steering gear got out of order. The engines were stopped and the boat began to roll heavily. In a little while many became seasick and there was a rush for the rails. The machine was repaired by ten o'clock; it was our first and only case of trouble with the ship.

One afternoon an orthodox betrothal party was held on the fore deck. The affianced couple were both orthodox *Chalutzim*. The groom-to-be, a serious looking fellow with spectacles, was twenty-two; his fiancée, Bella Gutfriend, was also twenty-two. She was all blushes and looked as though she would faint with pleasure when the traditional plate was broken at the end of the ceremony. I was an honored guest since I had been asked to use my influence to obtain a plate from the galley for the party. Both young people were Polish Jews who had met at a *hachsharah*.

The bride's father, a short, bearded Jew, all smiles in his shirtsleeves, black mohair vest, gold watch chain, and *yarmelka*, was the only relative present. The ceremony was performed by the leader of this orthodox group, a fine looking man named Moses Lieberman from Carpatho-Russia who had fought as a Czech officer on the Russian front for two and a half years. He said his grandmother was an aunt of Adolf Zuckor, the film magnate.

After the ceremony everybody danced the *hora*. The dancing and singing went on for the rest of the afternoon. One of the songs was a Hebrew song set to the tune of *Onward Christian Soldiers*.

At 4:30 o'clock the afternoon of the sixth day out all passengers were summoned to a meeting on the foredeck. They were addressed from the bridge by a *Haganah* worker. He gave them instructions about how they should act if they were captured and questioned by the British. There were cheers and applause when he said:

"As far as we are concerned, you are already citizens of *Eretz Israel*, whatever the English say."

He warned that there were still many difficulties ahead, but one of his warnings created a reaction that seemed natural to all of us.

"For a while you may find that you have not gone to *Eretz,* but to a prison in *Eretz."*

There was a burst of relieved laughter. Prison didn't matter so long as it was a prison in *Eretz.*

"There you'll see barbed wire again," he continued.

There were chuckles of satisfaction from the crowd. Barbed wire didn't matter either.

The meeting and the instructions caused a stir. Everybody felt that the end of our journey must be near.

We were told to line up on deck and proceed one by one to the captain's cabin, where we would be given our illegal immigration certificates.

We each filled out a blue certificate printed in Hebrew on one side and in English on the other. It was called, "Permit To Enter Palestine." We wrote in our name, the names of our parents, the place and date of our birth, and our nationality by birth. The certificate stated that we "had been found qualified by the representatives of the Jewish Community of Palestine for repatriation to *Eretz Israel."*

The certificate cited four authorities for the Jewish community's action.

The first was from Ezekiel: "And they shall abide in the lands that I have given unto Jacob my servant, wherein your fathers abode, and they shall abide therein, even they, and their children, and their children's children, forever."

The second was from Isaiah: "With great mercies will I gather thee."

The third was *Lord Balfour's Declaration of 2 November 1917,* and the last was *The Mandate for Palestine.*

The underground worker, who had a sense of humor, signed the name "Reb Moishe Ben Maimon" in the space for the signature of the quarantine officer. Moses ben Maimon, known also by his Latin name of Maimonides, was a famous Hebrew philosopher and physician of the Middle Ages.

The next afternoon we sighted smoke rising as if from another ship behind a little island far to the east. Everybody was sent below. When we came up again we saw that the ship had steamed from behind the island and was on the horizon ahead of us. We heard that it was a Turkish ship. Ours seemed to be following it. We did not know then that this was to be our first and last Sabbath eve on the ship, or that this other boat was to play an eventful part in our lives.

In the captain's cabin, the evening Sabbath candles burned and orthodox women blessed the candles with the traditional prayers. After dinner the foredeck was given over to the orthodox Jews for Sabbath services. A few in the crew joined them. The rest of us stood on the bridge watching. It was a moving scene.

We were headed due east. The light of the setting sun fell on the gray, blue, and gold of the prayer shawls as the pious among our passengers prayed and chanted, bowing over and over again to the east, where lay the Promised Land.

The next morning the Sabbath sky was blue and cloudless. Services were held on deck again, and as a special honor the captain and the underground *Haganah* emissary were called up to read the *Torah*. The captain was called up as the hero and he read the *Maftir,* the regular weekly portion from the prophets. The *Maftir* that morning had special significance for all of us. It was 66 Isiah 13, and those who understood Hebrew wept as they heard the words of the ancient prophecy:

"As one whom his mother comforteth, so will I comfort ye; and ye shall be comforted in Jerusalem."

IX

We were all ordered to pack our bags and have them ready the first thing in the morning. The order sent a thrill of excitement through the ship. That night everybody seemed to be singing. We all assumed that the sudden instructions meant that we would land in Palestine the next day.

On the foredeck the *Chalutzim* danced a tremendous *hora.* They joined hands and swung around the deck, stamping out the beat and leaping with joy until it seemed that they would crash through the deck. I could bear to watch no longer and broke into the circle between two of my friends and danced with them. We danced until we were exhausted.

On the pretext that it was the birthday of a sweet-faced German-Jewish girl named Frieda, who was the hardest working of all the volunteers in the galley, the crew were invited to a surprise party in the mess. We all sang Happy

Birthday, but we soon learned that the birthday was a subterfuge and that this was really a farewell to the ship.

Cake and coffee were served. The people sang Hebrew songs. I don't understand Hebrew and kept begging all evening that they sing some of the Yiddish songs I had heard on the way to Bratislava. Finally one of the *shomrim* explained:

"Those songs are too sad and bitter. They are the songs of the exile. Don't ask us to sing them. These Hebrew songs are the songs of our new life."

The Palestinian emissary sang a love song in Arabic which he had learned from Arab neighbors. They listened entranced. This, too, was Palestine for them.

When I went on deck the next morning I saw the other boat a few hundred yards away from us. It was a wooden freighter flying the Turkish flag. The name *Akbel II* and its home port, Istanbul, were painted on its stern. The refugees saw it with surprise. Soon word spread that we were to transfer to this other ship for the final leg of our journey.

The *Akbel,* a 250-ton freighter about half the length of our boat, was to tie up to us for the transfer. She maneuvered like a nervous old woman. Her captain ran excitedly up and down her bridge. His little mustache and his jerky movements made him look like Charlie Chaplin in an old-fashioned movie short. He had a whistle in his mouth and kept blowing on it and waving his arms for no apparent reason. His empty ship rode high in the water and rolled badly. Her deck would be now higher, now lower than ours.

While our passengers threw their luggage on our fore-deck the two ships moved back and forth, trying to get into position to tie up. At one time we touched, at another we actually caught ropes thrown from the fore and aft of the other ship. But each time we had to move away again. Once we bumped with a crash that damaged the port side of the Turkish boat. Her captain began shouting.

Our captain ran up on the bridge with a megaphone and yelled:

"Do you speak English?"

"Yes, I speak English," the other answered, but attempts at further conversation disclosed that this was about the limit of his English vocabulary.

The big Greek who was a pastry maker was summoned to the bridge and given the megaphone.

"Parlez Grec?" he shouted.

A man who seemed to be the first mate of the other boat shouted back:

"Oui! Oui!"

A conversation in Greek followed, with their first mate translating to the Turkish captain. On our bridge a Belgian translated the Greek Jew's French for our captain.

We learned that the Turkish captain was unwilling to risk tying up for fear our steel hull might stove in the side of his ship. He complained that his port side forward had already been damaged. It also became apparent that the Turkish captain was ready to call the whole deal off. He didn't seem anxious to take us on board.

The Turkish captain suddenly blew three blasts on his whistle, as though in farewell.

Nine of our huskiest men, including several ex-Partisans, climbed down the ladder into the motor launch we had lowered. One of them had a Jewish flag which he folded under his jacket. The others had pockets which bulged interestingly. We saw them reach the other ship and clamber up on its deck. Two men ran aft, one forward. The other six went on the bridge, and in a moment the Turkish captain and his first mate were surrounded.

What happened after that must have been pretty persuasive because from then on one of our men seemed to be in command. We could see another refugee arguing forcibly with two seamen on the deck of the other ship. They finally lowered one of the two lifeboats from the Turkish ship and began rowing toward us.

Both were barefoot and thin. One wore a ragged beret, the other looked as though his hair hadn't been combed since the Young Turk revolution. The one with the beret must have been a stoker. His face was as soot black as if he were made up for a minstrel show. Bright, intelligent, and friendly eyes twinkled out of the black face.

Blackface reached up a long oar which one of our sailors caught. The first of our men passengers began to climb down our ladder and into the boat. The transfer had begun.

The men were to go first, the women to follow later, with the sick and the doctor last of all. The women and the sick were lying all over the foredeck and the luggage. Some of them were very weak that morning and more than a little frightened at the prospect of that transfer on the open sea. The men waited aft and below deck, lining up in turn at the head of the ladder. On the other side, amidship, the doctor sat by the rail superintending his little corps of Red *Mogen Dovid* workers, who kept running back and forth to help the sick. The doctor looked pretty sick himself.

Neither the crew nor the passengers had had breakfast that morning. One of the latter asked me if I could please get something for his wife who was feeling faint. I went down to the galley. Below deck everything was in confusion and the odor was terrific. Several people had fainted and were stretched out near the gangway.

I found hot coffee in a big restaurant type percolator. I poured myself a cup. It tasted good. I poured a pitcherful of the hot coffee, took some of the cups and put a loaf of bread under one arm. One of the nurses helped me give out coffee to those who looked sick, and I tore off pieces of bread for those who were hungry.

The doctor was green around the gills and I went back and got a glass of coffee for him and a chocolate bar I found in one of the drawers in the galley. I mixed powdered milk with water and carried a pitcher full of milk to the sick women. One gray-haired woman who was seasick asked for a lemon, but I learned there were only five left and that these had to be saved for our trip on the other boat. Some of the women became alarmed when we put lifebelts on them for the transfer. The atmosphere was like that of a shipwreck.

There was a cry of "Man overboard!" and we saw a man swimming toward the other ship. Halfway there he was picked up by a lifeboat and brought back. He was a young

Belgian who angrily claimed that he had permission to swim to the other ship.

The women began to climb down the ladder. Their courage was amazing. Some of them had to jump into the arms of the sailors. One of our American crew members, an ex-soldier, said:

"What it took amphibious troops weeks to learn, these folks are doing without griping right off."

An elderly Jewish woman made a similar comment, with great satisfaction:

"It looks as though Jews can still do things."

When I went up on the bridge to say good-by to the crew I heard that the baggage was not to be transferred. The transfer was taking longer than was counted on and it was feared we might be caught by a British patrol boat. We were only about a hundred miles from Palestine.

I protested that our people should have been told this the night before. I said it didn't matter about their clothes, but that many refugees had put photographs and other precious mementoes of their vanished families in their baggage. I knew how much these faded photographs of wives, mothers, and children meant to them. In most cases it was all they had left of their old lives. I was told that the bags would have to be thrown overboard since that mountain of luggage was bound to raise suspicion if seen by a British patrol boat or plane. I begged the crew to at least take out photographs and letters before throwing the bags over.

"You'll have time this afternoon, after we leave," I pleaded. "It would be like a second death for these people to throw such mementoes away. Almost all these bags have names on them, but if you haven't time just dump all such personal things into one big bag and send them later to Palestine where these people can come and claim them."

They promised to do what they could.

I went off with the doctor and a boatload of sick women at 11:35. One woman cried in fright as we sped across the water. The last of the *shomrim* followed us to the Turkish boat and after that the crew brought huge crates with our lunches and some water. This took several trips.

I thought the transfer was completed when the motor launch arrived with a surprise—the boys were bringing our bags. It took an hour and half a dozen trips in the launch to transfer the baggage, and the crew members sweated like stevedores in the hot sun as they threw the bags on our deck.

Our passengers looked relieved to see their baggage. But it looked as though this transfer of baggage would prove disastrous. For just as the launch arrived with the last of the bags a warship came over the horizon to the north of us.

There was a cry from the launch:

"Let's get the hell outa here."

We all waved and cheered, but we watched anxiously as the launch sped across the four hundred yards or more that separated our two ships.

The warship, looming ever larger, bore down upon us. It looked as though all was lost.

X

I have never seen anything which seemed quite as large as that warship, its gray, menacing bulk growing ever larger, its huge guns pointed directly at us.

We could see the motor launch, in a final burst of speed, reach the ship on which we had sailed. We could see tiny figures clamber up the rope like monkeys on a vine. We watched others haul the launch on deck. And then the ship went off due west at a fast clip, like a swift hare running from a giant hound.

On our little Turkish cargo boat, a bell rang. The ancient engines turned and we started off in the opposite direction, due east. The worn timber creaked and the ship shook as her engines strained. Our maximum speed was about seven knots. It was like being in one of those nightmares in which one can barely move one's feet in flight from an advancing menace.

Since the two illegal vessels were going in opposite directions, our pursuer had to choose between us. We hoped the oncoming warship would set off after us. The boat we were on was a worthless old tub which had little chance of running the British blockade successfully anyway. The ship we had left was a swift and valuable vessel for which other refugees were already waiting in a south European port.

For a minute it looked as though the warship was heading for our first boat. We raised the *Mogen Dovid* to the top of our mast and then pulled it down again in the hope that this disclosure of our identity as a Jewish refugee ship would bring the warship in pursuit. It did, but not for the reason we expected. As the great ship headed across our bow, her decks crowded with sailors, we saw the flag of another great nation flying from her mast aft. Our tense refugees broke into a tremendous cheer. There was a great waving of hats and shouting of greetings across the water.

The warship was a big supercruiser. The British have begun to place protests with every nation which shows any friendliness to Jewish refugees trying to get to Palestine, and I do not want to create any difficulties for that naval commander or his country. But I don't imagine he was ever cheered so enthusiastically as he was that day by our refugees.

The ship from which we had transferred reached the western horizon and stopped as if to see what was happening to us. When the warship resumed her course our old ship started up again and in a few minutes disappeared over the horizon. The warship went south and also vanished over the horizon.

Our little freighter was alone on that vast and ancient sea. She plowed along wearily, her engines wheezing like an asthmatic old woman. Her hull was low in the water from the weight of her unusual cargo. Her main deck and her three small upper decks, fore, aft, and amidships, were packed as tightly with people as a rush-hour subway. Sick and exhausted women had even invaded the wheelhouse and were lying all over its floor and on the back bench and around the feet of the harassed Turkish pilot. The wheelhouse was the only cool spot on the ship.

Amidships there was an ancient salon with a galley in which our precious supply of water was stored and guarded. Off the entrance to the salon was a water closet, the only one on the ship. It stank heartily. The dingy, dark, and unfurnished salon beyond was filled with people. Even the grimy stokehold in which two profusely sweating and blackened stokers were at work was filled with refugees, their faces pale and drawn.

The worst places of all on the ship were the two cargo holds. In these holds, 'tween decks had been newly built to increase the amount of passenger space. The holds were open to the sky. The 'tween decks provided a kind of balcony around them, just high enough for refugees to sit in them. The only air and light came from the opening on deck. Inside, the holds were dark, dank, and fearfully hot, much more like a den for wild animals than a habitation for human beings. One narrow ladder led down into each hold. A guard stood on deck at the top of the ladder. His function became clearer as that hot and cloudless summer day wore on.

To move around the ship was a slow and painful job. One did not try it often. One had to climb over people sitting or lying on the deck. It was hard to avoid stepping on them. They lay exhausted and irritable from the fierce heat. All were hungry and thirsty.

It was after three before the guards could open the crates containing food and water. There was an emergency lunch packed in separate paper bags for each one of us.

The galley crew on the old ship must have stayed up all night preparing those lunches.

For the orthodox, the lunch bag contained a hardtack jelly sandwich made of two pieces of big round biscuit smeared with grape jelly. The biscuits were so hard they had to be broken on the rail. There was a handful of currants and a big bar of chocolate. The non-kosher packages also had a bar of chocolate, two pieces of hardtack and a big slice of bologna in place of the jelly. We tackled the lunches with famished zest. This was the only food we were to have for two days and nights.

While we were eating, the *shomrim* passed around with big cans of water, the kind of cans stowed away on lifeboats for use in case of shipwreck. We all got a few sips from the dirty glasses carried by the guards and passed from hand to hand. The water was warm and stale, but to us it tasted good.

I had squeezed into a place near the doctor and his wife on the upper deck amidships. We sat with our backs against the hatch which provided a little air for the hot noisome stokehold below. Every once in a while one of the stokers, his face black with soot, would climb up for a bit of air and sit grinning like a cheerful bogeyman at the girls. The stokers never opened their mouths throughout the voyage. I suppose they spoke only Turkish, but they might have been deaf mutes as far as we were concerned.

That Turkish freighter might have been a fine boat in the days of Abdul Hamid, but its engines now shook as if they would break down any minute. It was horribly overloaded and leaned crazily in the water whenever there were more people on one side than the other.

We had to make a fateful decision. Should we try to run the British blockade, or should we ask for help? The *Haganah* emissary on board was afraid that some mishap might capsize or sink the ship with all aboard. The British blockading forces by that time on the sea and in the air were so numerous that even a faster ship could hardly hope to land its cargo secretly in Palestine. He decided it would be best to send out an SOS and give ourselves up voluntarily to the British rather than risk a disaster.

The SOS went out over the portable wireless we had brought on board. Distress flags were raised. Shortly before five o'clock a two-engined plane zoomed out of the east and flew so low over our boat that it created a welcome passing breeze. It circled and recircled around us. A little later a four-engined plane repeated the same performance. After dark, patrol planes dropped flares around the boat. But after the first flares no planes returned and we were left alone and apprehensive on that dark and gloomy sea.

That night was the worst I had yet spent. I was to learn that night, and to learn the hard and feverish way, what life in a concentration camp had been like.

We had no more food and little water left. We feared that at any moment the frightfully overloaded boat might capsize or sink. Our SOS seemed to have been to no avail. Though British planes had circled the afternoon and dropped red flares around us shortly after sunset, there was no further sign of help that night on the dark and lonely sea. We thought we were about one hundred miles from Palestine and we assumed that we were headed in that direction. We were to learn differently in the morning.

The most terrible problem of all that night was to get the men to take turns going down into the hold. There wasn't enough space on the decks of the ship to accommodate all of us. We had to take turns. The holds were packed with men. Our *shomrim* were supposed to see that those in the hold were allowed to come up on deck every few hours and men on deck required to take their places below. A bitter battle went on constantly—not many men were willing to give up a place in the open air to go down into the unlighted, hot, and stinking hold.

A few went below voluntarily. Some went shamefaced after the guards had explained and pleaded. But some sat silent and stubborn while the *shomrim* cried hoarsely, furiously, and impotently for men to go below. I heard one cry in Yiddish, *"Chaverim, Ich red zu menschen, nit behemos"* ("Comrades, I am talking to men, not beasts"). Another pleaded, *"Ich hab nit kein revolver, ich red zu eich als menschen."* ("I don't have a revolver, I'm pleading with you as men.") But with many, all pleas were unavailing. Some had to be picked up bodily and carried to the hold. Fist fights broke out.

I was on the upper deck. A *shomer* came up the ladder looking for men who were not too ill to be sent below. He yanked a big blond German-looking fellow to his feet. But the latter, his face livid, shouted:

"I was in that hold all day long when others were on deck. I can't stand it any more. I swear by my mother that if you try to take me down there I'll strangle you with my own hands."

He raised his hands as if to grab the *shomer's* throat. He looked mad enough to do so. The *shomer* backed down.

The scene from the upper deck might have been something out of the Inferno. The deck was dimly lit. In the center of the deck was the entrance to the hold. It sounded as though a riot were in progress below. Big fat Rudy, the ex-circus strong man, who was leader of the *shomrim*, fought his way about on deck, naked to the waist. He had a whistle in his mouth and alternately blew sharp blasts and issued hoarse shouts of command as he superintended the transfer of men from the deck to the hold. The engines beat regularly and interminably like the tom-toms of a heathen god to whom we were all waiting to be sacrificed, and the mass of struggling men below seemed to be a kind of weird and hellish ballet.

I was a privileged character, allowed the run of the ship and a place on the upper deck. I had climbed to a seat on the boom where I could hold on to the mast and get a good view of the ship and the sea. But I felt like a slacker and so climbed down on the lower deck and pushed my way through the quarreling men to the guards at the opening of the hold.

"It's the journalist," somebody yelled.

"He doesn't have to go down there," Rudy shouted hoarsely.

But I said I wanted to take my turn with the rest and Rudy let me climb down the ladder into the hold.

At the foot of the ladder men were fighting for a chance to climb up. I forced my way through the tight-packed crowd to a place where I could sit against the far wall. When one got used to it, the darkness was not complete. A faint red glow came through the opening. It was frightfully hot. I fought and pushed for room in which to strip to the waist. The air was sickening, the noise almost unbearable; the sensible thing was to sit and sweat and keep quiet.

The people around me were hot and angry and irritable and not at all friendly. In that dark and noisy dungeon nobody had the strength to think of anything but himself. There was a constant milling about as new people arrived from the deck and others already below tried to fight their way back to the foot of the ladder. A newcomer pushed his way over to me and yelled with a curse that I was sitting on his bag and that I had his place. He was beside himself with rage over being sent back into the hold. He scared me. I got up and pushed my way through to another part of the hold where I squeezed in along the wall among other snarling, irritable shipmates.

The heat, noise, and bad air drained away the strength of all but the strongest and fiercest. These gradually pushed and fought their way to the center under the opening while the weaker were left sitting or standing in the darker, almost airless, sections under the 'tween decks. Those at the foot of the ladder fought among themselves to stay there and tried to climb up. The guard kept push-

ing them down; there was a violent interchange of blows
and curses.

A few of the cleverer, stronger, and more unscrupulous
seemed to get back on deck after less than ten minutes
below. But some had been in that hold for hours, and a
few in the darkest far corners may well have been there
since they came on board. They seemed too utterly spent
to move. A kind of fierce Darwinian struggle went on in
that hold and in that struggle the men seemed to become
less than human. It was like being in a den of wolves.

I spent almost two hours in the hold and then began
to struggle and push forward to get my hands and feet
on that coveted ladder. I had had enough. To breathe the
fresh air and to see the stars again even from that incred-
ibly crowded and dirty deck was a relief no words can
adequately describe. It was as though one had emerged
from a prison or a concentration camp. I imagined that
this was how men fought and snarled in a *katzet*. I later
asked friends on board and they told me that the spirit
and atmosphere of the hold was that of concentration
camps in which they had been. The *katzet* bred a sub-
human individualism. Everyone had to fight for sleeping
space, for bread, for a breath of air, for life itself.

On deck I ran into a German psychologist friend who
had also been in the hold. I had never seen a man's face
so changed in a few hours. He looked exhausted. His face
was drawn, one eye was strained and out of focus. The
pleasant young man I knew had the look of a creature
cowering under oppression. He must have looked that way
when he was in Buchenwald.

I confess with shame that I never again volunteered to
go down into the hold. It was more than I could take. I
felt shaky when I came up on deck and begged one of
the *shomrim* to haul up a bucket of sea water and throw
it over me as I leaned far over the rail. The shock of the
cold water was delicious and refreshing and I begged for
another shower. Afterwards I went up on the upper deck.
The doctor and his wife made room for me under the
boom. I slept there sitting up.

I got up around four and climbed up on the boom. The
sky was growing light. At 4:35 the red sun rose out of
the sea to disclose two surprises. There were high mountains on our left which I thought must be the mountains
of Lebanon, but they turned out to be those of Cyprus.
Our Turkish captain, perhaps losing his nerve, had been
taking us away from Palestine.

The second surprise, about a mile away on our star-
board side, was a British destroyer. It was waiting to close
in on us like a grayhound of the sea.

XI

We were about eighty miles farther from our goal than
we had been at the point of transfer.

We didn't know what the attitude of the British would
be. We hoped that the destroyer had come in answer to
our SOS, that they would take a few of our sick on board

their ship, perhaps give us some food and water and tow us into Haifa. Perhaps we had too high an opinion of British gallantry.

The British moved closer and we read that the number of this destroyer was R-75 and its name the *Virago*. When it came alongside one of the *shomrim* handed me a megaphone and asked me to talk to the British.

"Hullo, hullo! We're in a bad way. Can you give us a tow to Haifa?" I shouted across the water.

Sailors on the deck of the destroyer pulled the cover off a lifeboat and lowered it into the sea. Six sailors and an ensign got into the boat and began to row toward our ship. Aboard they made their way gingerly to the wheel house. Many people lay underfoot, too sick or exhausted to move. The British sailors stepped over them carefully. They wore white shorts. Their officer, a fledgling ensign, tried hard to look imperturbable.

"Who's spokesman for these people?" the officer asked me.

"*Ich kenn nit reden English* (I can't speak English)," I answered in Yiddish.

I was taking no chances on being taken off that boat by the British before I could reach Palestine. I waved my hand to my German friend. He spoke a rather awkward English with a strong Dutch accent. He had learned English in Holland before the war.

I have never seen a more complicated bit of linguistics than the interrogation of our Turkish captain by the British ensign. The ensign spoke English with that calm assurance Englishmen seem to have abroad that they will of course be understood. It took a chain of translators, however, to make this possible.

The ensign spoke to my German friend in English. The German translated this into Hebrew. One of our Greeks stood by and interpreted the Hebrew into broken Russian for one of the Turkish sailors, who, in turn, translated for the Turkish captain.

One of the British sailors stood at the top of the wheel house with two signal flags. In his white shorts, bare knees and brown, heavy socks he looked like an enlarged Boy Scout. His name, satisfyingly enough, turned out to be Popham.

Another sailor with a message pad stood beside the ensign. They were surrounded by an unwashed horde of refugees, your correspondent included.

The ensign, flustered by the stares of the women, some of whom didn't look too unattractive even on that dreadful morning, handed a knife to the sailor with which to sharpen a stub of a pencil. He proceeded to dictate the results of his interrogation.

The sailor wrote it all down respectfully, rereading it aloud for the benefit of Popham, who signaled it across the water to the destroyer. The ensign dictated, much like a businessman in an office, pausing nervously over his choice of words. At one point his youthful upper class dignity broke down completely and he shouted to the sailor on the wheelhouse:

"Did you get that, Pop?"

But otherwise he addressed him as "Pop'm."

The most important question asked by the ensign was

whether we were willing voluntarily to be towed into Haifa. There was a good reason for this question. We were outside Palestinian territorial waters. Under international law the British have no right to seize a boat on the high seas, even if they know for a certainty that it is carrying unauthorized immigrants to Palestine. On two occasions the British have been ordered by their own courts in Palestine to return Jewish ships captured on the high seas. On the other hand, if an illegal boat voluntarily submits to British jurisdiction on the high seas the seizure is of course a legal one.

We told the ensign that we were willing to submit to British authority and asked him to tow us into Haifa.

The ensign dictated to the destroyer, "Severe engine trouble, plus overcrowding, made it impossible to proceed," and that we would place ourselves voluntarily under British authority to be towed in. A big signal lamp on the destroyer twinkled back a question:

"Is there enough food and water on board?"

The ensign answered that we were out of both, and stood nervously twiddling his pencil against his pants under the stares of the numb and savage horde surrounding him. He was thin, blond, of somewhat more than medium height. He looked the picture of a well-bred English boy of good family. He was obviously distressed by our plight. My friends and I liked him.

The ensign asked whether we had a towline aboard. We hadn't. Then he asked if we could clear the foredeck so that a towline could be attached to our boat. *Shomrim* made their way slowly and painfully to the foredeck to clear a path, but with little success.

The foredeck was packed tight with girls and women. They had slept leaning against each other. The lucky ones had sat all night at the railing, their feet hanging over the water. They were dazed, sleepy, tired, and resentful. Each was afraid to move lest she lose her precious space.

I megaphoned an appeal to them in my rather inadequate Yiddish.

"Comrades," I pleaded, "the British officer on board is a kind man and he is offering to tow us into Haifa. That means we can be in *Eretz* this evening. You must clear the foredeck so that a towline can be attached to the British destroyer. Please move and make place so that when the British sailors come back on board they will have room."

A few began to move off the upper deck and down the rail. Some of those on the deck below should have moved into the cargo hold and made room for the women from the upper deck, and some did. But the hold itself was jammed with men clamoring for a chance to get up into the light and air.

In the meantime the ensign and his six sailors climbed back into the lifeboat in which they had come and started back to the destroyer. We watched them hopefully. We were hungry and thirsty and hoped for food and water.

The *shomrim* were busy on both decks, forcing men into the hold and bringing women down from the foredeck. It looked as though the English would save us after all.

We were in for an unpleasant surprise. We saw the ensign and the six sailors go aboard the destroyer. Then we saw tiny figures hoisting the lifeboat on board. We wondered why, since a boat would be needed to bring us food and water.

The destroyer began to move and for one relieved moment we thought it was maneuvering into position to attach a towline to our cargo boat. But the distance between us widened. The destroyer sailed off to the east.

This destruction of our hopes was so unexpected that our reaction was one of dulled amazement rather than indignation. No one shouted or cursed or shook a fist at the vanishing British destroyer. We just watched it in silence. The destroyer grew smaller and smaller and finally vanished over the horizon.

"It will be a miracle if we ever get to *Eretz*," the doctor said.

XII

The second day and night on the Turkish cargo boat were the worst I ever spent. The British destroyer steamed off shortly after 7 A.M. without giving us food and water or the tow into Haifa for which we had asked. We were to the south of Cyprus, about 180 miles from Palestine. The sky was cloudless and the sea calm but the day was brutally hot.

The boat from which we had transferred on the seas early the previous morning had given us water and provisions for but one day. Had our Turkish captain sailed straight for Palestine we would have reached there that night. Either he had lost his way or his nerve and headed north instead of east. We were eighty miles further away from Palestine than we had been at our transfer point.

Some people on board still had the remains of the lunch bag given us the day before but there was very little water; all we had were a few precious and closely guarded regulation cans of water, the kind packed on lifeboats in case of shipwreck, and it was over water that our first crisis that day was to arise.

The heat was sickening. There were a score or more of people on board, including four pregnant women and a cardiac case who had to be given injections at regular intervals. The doctor was on the upper deck amidships with a small store of medicines. He was ill himself, and our *Red Mogen Dovid* (Jewish Red Cross) workers would come to him during the day for medicines and instructions.

On the lower deck one of the *shomrim* had attached a rope to a bucket and given showers to those who wanted them. The men would strip to the waist and lean far over the side. A *shomrim* would pull up a bucket of water and throw it over them. I had one every hour or so during the day. The shock of the cold water was very refreshing.

I got another bucket and tied a rope to it and had one of the *shomrim* fill it and hand it up to the top deck amidships, where there were many men and women sick with the heat and thirst. I went around with the bucket

sprinkling water over the needy and wetting handker-
chiefs so people could put them on their foreheads. The
women didn't like the shock of the water; the men did,
even one sick old man I called *zeida* (grandpa) but who
told me he had neither children nor grandchildren.

The men stretched blankets as awnings against the sun.
People lay down under the lifeboats where there was a bit
of shade and even around the hot smokestack. Most of
them were too miserable to think of anyone but themselves.

Tempers wore very thin on the boat. It was difficult to
keep a way open to the wheelhouse and to make people
take turns in the hot hold. One *shomer* said to me in
exasperation, *"Juden und pferd seinen die selbe sach—
beide muss men treiben."* ("Jews and horses are the same
thing—you have to drive both of them.") I'm afraid I
lost my temper several times and I apologize to those of
my comrades whose feelings I may have hurt.

At one point I was trying to make room on the star-
board side amidships for a sick woman. A boy of about
twelve was sitting there. I asked him to give up his place.
He refused, and a woman near him whom I took to be
his mother looked indignantly at me. I yanked him to his
feet, shouting:

"What do you mean you won't give your place to a
sick woman. If you don't want to be a *mensch* (man)
don't go to *Eretz.*"

The word *mensch* is richer in Yiddish than in English
and has a richer connotation of manliness.

The boy moved away resentfully, but later I saw him

helping to put up a blanket as an awning and shouting to another boy:

"Come on, help! If you want to go to *Eretz* you must be a *mensch*."

"Now you're acting like a real *Chalutz*," I said, patting him on the back.

In my water-soaked notebook for that day there is this notation:

"I feel sick. No water yet today. I found a piece of hardtack under the boom. Someone else had eaten part of it. I chewed on the rest with relish. I had an odd experience I have read about in stories of shipwreck. The hardtack did not dissolve or even grow wet in my mouth. I had no saliva. It pulverized, and I swallowed it dry."

The one cool spot on the boat was the wheelhouse. I had a nap there in the afternoon, and found an opened tin of concentrated lifeboat rations. I ate a biscuit and a chocolate tablet and had a tiny mouthful of brackish water from a very dirty glass. I rinsed my mouth with the water before swallowing. It might have been nectar, it tasted so delicious.

Four sick women were lying on the floor around the wheelhouse.

The shortage of water precipitated a crisis in the afternoon. There was a terrific fight on the lower deck and a lot of shouting. Rudy jumped on the stairs leading to the afterdeck and yelled:

"I take over all power on this boat and order the *shomrim* to distribute the rest of the water."

He was finally calmed down, but not until he was

promised that one of our last remaining cans of water
would be passed around.

I felt guilty that evening because of a special treat. I
was near the wheelhouse and looked in to see the Turkish
captain in his pajamas eating his dinner and drinking tea.
The crew had a small store of food and a spirit lamp with
which they prepared tea. I looked at the tea so longingly
that he invited me to have a cup. It was hot and sweet and
I have never tasted anything quite so good. I insisted on
giving him one of my last packs of Camels in return.

That night there was a panic. The barometer began to
fall. There was a dead calm on the sea, as if before a
storm. About eleven o'clock the captain became alarmed
He was afraid the boat would capsize in a storm. His
fear spread to the *shomrim* who began to herd people off
the decks and into the holds. Fights broke out and women
became hysterical. Word spread that a storm was coming
and that the boat might sink. Even some of the best of
the women *Chalutzim* lost their nerve.

We sent out an SOS. About two in the morning a
British destroyer came alongside. It turned floodlights on
us and we saw the number R-75 on its sides, the same
number as the boat which had refused us aid the previous
morning.

I handled the megaphone:

"Is that the *Virago?*"

I repeated the question, but again got no answer.

We asked how far we were from Haifa.

"Thirty-five miles," was the reply.

"The barometer's falling," I shouted, "and our captain

is afraid that we may go under in a storm. We're terribly
overloaded. Could you take some of our sick people on
board and give us a tow to Haifa?"

We waited but got no answer.

"Won't you please answer?" I asked. There was no
answer.

I tried again.

"Won't you please answer?"

There was no reply this time either.

The captain had shut off our engines and the whole
ship waited anxiously for some response.

"Won't you please answer?" I asked for the third time.

But they remained silent.

One of the *shomrim* standing near me said:

"The hell with the bastards."

We waited about fifteen minutes. I picked up the megaphone and shouted derisively,

"Thank you."

We started up our engines to a full six or seven knots
and started off for Haifa.

In spite of our fears and a rough sea, we avoided a
storm. Shortly before dawn I slept for a while on top of
the wheelhouse. I woke to see the dim outlines of a mountain toward the southeast.

As the light increased and the sun rose, a cry ran over
the ship.

"It's *Eretz Israel.*"

We saw Mount Carmel ahead of us, and the town of
Haifa sleeping in the morning sun below us. In the harbor

as we came in we saw what seemed to be a whole British fleet waiting for us.

The refugees cheered and began to sing *Hatikvah,* the Jewish national anthem. We pulled down the Turkish flag at our helm and raised the *Mogen Dovid* and the Union Jack side by side. People jumped for joy, kissed and hugged each other on the deck.

So singing we moved into the arms of the waiting British, in *Eretz* at last.

XIII

I must give the British credit for a bit of gallantry on our entrance into Haifa harbor. The same destroyer, R-75, the HMS *Virago,* which had twice refused us aid, was the warship assigned to take us over in the harbor. A small boat with six men and an officer, but not the same young ensign who had been on board before, came out from the *Virago* and was followed by another boatload of Palestinian Arab police.

The officer, with the Palestinian Arabs in their lambskin hats clearing a way for him, first went to the wheelhouse and said: "I take possession of this ship." Then he ordered a sailor to change the flag at our foremast. There on entering the harbor we had pulled down the Turkish flag and raised the *Mogen Dovid* — the blue-and-white Jewish flag—side by side with the Union Jack.

Much to our surprise the British did not pull down the Jewish flag but only the Union Jack. The Union Jack we had raised was the merchant marine Union Jack, the Union Jack on a field of red. That was the proper flag for us as a merchant vessel, albeit illegal. In taking possession the British replaced our Union Jack with the Royal Ensign and allowed us to proceed into Haifa with our Jewish flag flying.

So we moved closer to frizzly Mount Carmel, with stucco-colored Haifa on its northern flank. Watching our arrival were a half dozen warships in the harbor, and, far away along the docks, crowds of people. We felt proud and exultant to arrive with the Jewish flag at our mast.

The refugees looked for the first time upon the Holy Land with wondering and often tear-filled eyes. This was the sight for which they had longed with all their hearts, the sight for which they had risked their lives crossing one illegal border after another and on the high seas.

I was standing near the wheelhouse. The British officer stood beside me.

"I thought it was very sporting of us this morning to send up the Union Jack as well as the *Mogen Dovid*," I said. "But I must say I think you fellows were very sporting, too, to leave our *Mogen Dovid* up there when you raised your Royal Ensign."

The officer, a young and pleasant chap, smiled and said: "Well, we English are a sporting people."

Then, noticing my accent, he asked curiously:

"Have you ever been to America?"

He didn't ask whether I was an American. It must have

seemed too fantastic to him to expect an American to be on that boat. By that time, dirty and unshaven, I looked like the other DP's on board. I had no intention of being taken off until I was ready to go, so I only answered:

"Yes, I've been to America."

The British officer then broke some amazing news.

"You probably haven't heard," he said, "that there have been widespread raids in Palestine on the Jewish Agency and the leadership of the *Haganah*. Athlit, the detention camp to which refugees are usually taken, is full of Jewish leaders and you people will be held in the harbor."

When I heard this I decided to show my papers and try to get off the ship as soon as possible.

"In that case," I said, "I might as well show you my passport. I'm an American newspaperman and I had intended going along to Athlit so I could write about conditions inside the camp. But since we're to be held in the harbor I guess my mission's done and I might as well start for home."

I pulled out my green American passport and showed the British visa for Palestine which I had obtained at the British Embassy in Washington. The officer looked at them and then at me.

"Why the devil did you ever come on a tub like this?" he asked. "You must be the only legal passenger on board."

I said I was and explained that I came as a newspaperman in order to be able at write at first hand of the Jewish immigration to Palestine.

"Now that you know what conditions are like," the officer asked, "would you do it again?"

"Sure," I answered. "I had a wonderful time."

Some of my comrades stood listening curiously to this conversation. Then one of the girls voiced the only real fear that my fellow passengers felt. She said to me in Yiddish:

"Do you think the British might send us back?"

I translated the question for the officer and he smiled and said:

"No, we wouldn't do that. We British aren't that bad."

After I translated the answer to my relieved comrades the officer began to explain the British side of the matter.

"You people must realize," he said, "that the British are good friends of the Jews, but we have many other problems in our Empire and can't do everything we'd like to do."

This was before the British began forcibly removing illegal immigrants to Cyprus.

A police cutter came alongside and an officer asked in Hebrew how many sick we had aboard. The doctor told him there were about twenty-four and asked for help. A half hour later the cutter returned with a Palestinian-Jewish doctor and they began to remove the sick.

Water was brought aboard at ten o'clock. We passed down canteens to be filled for our sick, but no one paid too much attention to us. It was noon before we all had enough water.

Our boat had been renamed the *Beria,* in honor of the famous settlement the Jews had built up in Palestine that spring, in defiance of the British who had once razed it to the ground. The ship was taken into an inner part of the harbor, away from the town, and moored inside an artificial breakwater which was surrounded by a high iron fence. Eight illegal ships, including the *Sir Josiah,* were lined up there. We were transferred to the *Max Nordau,* which had brought a thousand immigrants from Rumania the month before.

An unpleasant surprise awaited us. On board the *Nordau* we were told that two cases of suspected bubonic plague had been found among the sick taken off the *Beria* and that we would be quarantined in the harbor for ten days or two weeks.

The *Max Nordau* was a change for the better. It was larger than the *Beria* and the decks were swept and clean.

Our people began to promenade the decks, chatting happily among themselves and gazing curiously at the land they had so hoped to see.

The Jewish community of Haifa sent food aboard: fresh white rolls, red tomatoes, and green peppers, white cream cheese, individual pint bottles of *laban,* the thick sour milk of the Levant, and big bunches of grapes.

Each of us was given a pint of *laban,* a big bunch of grapes, two rolls, a generous helping of the cheese, two tomatoes, and a pepper. The grapes were not quite in season and were very expensive. Their sweet juice and the cool *laban* were blissful food for parched throats after our long thirst. It must have cost a fortune to provide that lunch for us. It is no small matter to feed a thousand people and we were but one of the many thousands who had been arriving at that port since the war had ended. We ate heartily and gratefully.

But we were soon to find out that in some ways we had made a change for the worse. The *Max Nordau* was fitted out below deck with the same kind of temporary wooden bunks, four or five deep, on which we had slept on our first boat. The difference was that since the ship was lying idle in the harbor, with no steam up, there was no power to flush the bilges, to work the ventilators, or to provide current for the lights.

I got a rough wooden bunk with no mattress and several gaps in the wood. But I was one of the lucky ones, for my bunk was in an ancient stateroom on deck. It had a window and I shared it with only one person, a young *Red Mogen Dovid* worker, a Dutch boy named Perite. We had a washroom with a washstand but no water, and a small table. We felt among the privileged of the earth and invited our friends to take turns sleeping in the cabin during the day.

But the others were not so fortunate: to sleep below decks was sheer torture. There was a terrible odor from the unflushed latrines which pervaded the sleeping quarters. It was fearfully hot. At night there was a constant symphony of moans, sighs, whispered conversations. Few could sleep, and the refugees came on deck early in the morning looking haggard, bleary eyed, and at the end of their resources.

There was very little water and everyone felt the need of a wash. We begged for pint bottles of water from the galley or stood in long lines to fill our canteens at the slow-running tap below decks. The men had to shave out of pint bottles or canteens. The women tried their best to wash up a bit, and to comb their hair, but it was difficult to do after ten days without a bath.

So long as we had been on the way to *Eretz* the goal was enough to keep people's spirits up. But once we arrived, tantalizingly within sight of *Eretz,* yet not there, to be prisoners in what the refugees regarded as their homeland, to live in stink, filth and wretchedness, was more than the best of the *Chalutzim* could bear.

The assistant chief superintendent of the harbor, a British official, came on board and asked to see the American journalist. I showed him my passport and visa and he made a note of their numbers and said he was satisfied that I was a legal immigrant. But when I asked when I could leave, he said that was up to the medical authorities since the ship was in quarantine.

When a Palestinian-Jewish health officer came aboard later, he told me that I would have to stay on board with the others until the quarantine was lifted, which would be not less than ten days. I was lined up with the rest and given a shot in the arm for bubonic plague by a British doctor, who did a very skillful job, and treated us well.

I was determined to get off that boat. I did a little investigating of my own. Our refugee doctor told me that while the British were justified in taking all precautions, the two suspected cases of bubonic plague were not that at all but cases of swollen glands. He said the tests at the hospital in Haifa, as reported to him that morning by the health authorities, confirmed his diagnosis. He also said that with Athlit and other detention camps full of arrested Jewish leaders, the British would probably use quarantine as an excuse to keep us on the boat. I decided I was going.

The day before I had sat on deck too tired and beaten to move. I felt that if anyone tried to talk to me I'd burst into tears. But after a night's sleep, even on that wooden bunk, I felt chipper again. I got a bottle of water and shaved, and then another bottle and took a sponge bath. I found out that at seven in the evening a cutter would take the doctor and some others ashore. I would take a chance.

I put on my U. S. military correspondent's uniform in the afternoon, packed my bags and said good-by to my friends. Just before seven o'clock, when the cutter came alongside, I walked down the gangplank with my bags and got on the cutter.

Perhaps it was the uniform. Perhaps it was my manner, which took for granted that I was leaving. The doctor probably thought I had the permission of the military, and the military assumed that I had the permission of the doctor. Anyway, no one asked me any questions.

I'll never forget the farewell I got as the cutter moved away from the boat. Word had spread that I was going to try to get away and everybody was on deck to see me off. It had meant something to everybody's morale to have an American newspaper correspondent on board and I had made many friends. These Jews were my own people and I had come to love them on our long trip together.

They waved and cheered and cried *sholom.* I stood on the cutter among the rather startled Britishers on board and shouted *sholom* and threw kisses to my friends and comrades. They were fortunate, for they were among the last shiploads of illegal immigrants permitted to land. They were not sent to Cyprus. After a stay in Athlit detention camp, they were set free, and since returning home I have had happy letters from three of my friends of the voyage.

The cutter pulled away. The ship grew smaller and vanished. Haifa loomed up ahead of me. At the dock I walked off. The immigration offices were closed but I went through customs and out the gates. An Arab guard who knew the doctor who had come ashore with me gave us a friendly *sholom*.

My underground journey to Palestine had ended. I was in *Eretz* at last.

UNDERGROUND TO PALESTINE

Epilogue

Epilogue

I

When I reached Cairo after leaving Palestine I had luncheon with a group of friends I had made on my previous trip to the Middle East. The conversation turned, of course, to Palestine and the Jewish problem. Some of my friends have the Arab point of view, some the British. Some favored one supposed solution, some another. I found myself curiously uninterested in all their talk.

I had begun to feel like a DP myself on my underground trip to Palestine, and I found myself reacting like a DP during that luncheon debate. In presenting these conclusions to my trip, I hope I may be pardoned if in

231

taking leave of a memorable journey and memorable comrades I speak first as one of them.

For my comrades, for the Jews waiting in the DP camps of Germany and Austria, for the Jews fleeing across the borders of Eastern and Central Europe from new persecution, there is no longer a problem. Palestine is not a matter of theory.

Have they any choice? Is any country opening its doors to them? Has anything come of the endless conferences on refugees—the months of talk before the war, when many of the dead 6,000,000 might still have been saved; the endless negotiations and investigations since, when there are so few left?

Not all my comrades were heroes or idealists. Many of them would prefer life in a settled country like America or England to the hardships and struggle of the frontier in *Eretz*. But for most of them, Palestine is not merely the one possibility for a new life, is not merely a place of refuge, but *the country to which they want to go*. I met people in the DP camps and I talked with people on the boat who had relatives and affidavits for the U.S.A., but were going to Palestine instead.

Is this so hard to understand? They have been kicked around as Jews and now they want to live as Jews. Over and over again, I heard it said: "We want to build a Jewish country. . . . We are tired of putting our sweat and blood into places where we are not welcome. . . . We have wandered enough." These Jews want the right to live as a people, to build as a people, to make their contribution to the world as a people. Are their national aspirations any less worthy of respect than those of any other oppressed people?

I was impressed, on my underground voyage, with the vitality I found among these, my brethren from the East. What is the source of this vitality and strength? The source is twofold. The first lies in the Zionist idea, in this romantic dream of a Viennese journalist in the late nineteenth century, the dream of a Return. This has given them a goal, their lives a purpose, their shattered selves a focal point around which to reintegrate their personalities and to recover their moral health.

The second source of their strength is simpler. It is that lack of alternative to which I have already referred.

"For us," one of my friends had said to me on shipboard, "Palestine is the last stop. We can go no farther." They have nothing to lose, hardly life itself—for life for Jews in Poland and Rumania and Hungary today is too precarious to be worth much, and life in the DP camps is hardly life at all, but a kind of waiting day after day in an open grave, from which one may or may not arise.

Such people, in such a mood, are not easily defeated. They who knew the SS are not terrified by the British. They who saw the gas chambers are not frightened by a naval blockade. They are going to *Eretz.*

I say here what I said in private to Azzam Bey Pasha, head of the Arab League, over coffee in Cairo. I did not say it in defiance, for I respect Azzam Bey, and I would far rather deal with that Arab statesman and patriot on behalf of the Jews than with Ernest Bevin. I said it as a simple statement of fact when he asked what I thought of the current situation: *"Nothing will stop the people I traveled with from rebuilding a great Jewish community in Palestine."*

II

I came back convinced that the Jewish people can expect nothing whatsoever from the British government, except disappointment, betrayal, and attack. I say that with apologies to the good friends the cause of the DP's and of Palestine has in each of the three British parties in England and even among British officialdom in the Middle East.

I want to set down in all soberness the simple statement that the British Empire is now waging a war designed to smash what the Jews have accomplished in Palestine and to break the hearts of the homeless in the DP camps and elsewhere by shutting off their one hope—the so-called illegal immigration.

I say so-called illegal immigration because the only right Britain has to the control of Palestine and Trans-Jordan lies in a League of Nations mandate and a separate treaty with the United States giving Britain temporary trusteeship in order to establish a Jewish national home. To bar Jews from the Holy Land is to violate the mandate and the treaty.

I would not be reporting accurately if I left the impression that any such legalistic argument lies behind the

determined migration of my old comrades across dangerous frontiers and blockaded seas. The British Foreign
Office may consider this another bit of stubborn Jewish
foolishness, but Jews—who have long historical memories
—instinctively think of Palestine as a place in which they
have rights older than a League of Nations mandate, em-
bodied in a document which Christian Britain respects,
though sometimes only on Sunday.

When I was in Jerusalem, I was told in one of the best
informed sources in the Middle East that the British military had drawn up a three-part plan which was to culmi-
nate—if sufficient excuse could be found—in an offensive
operation designed to smash Jewish settlements and cities.
One high British military official told a Jewish leader
frankly—I assure the reader this is not just gossip—"The
world took the killing of six million Jews and if we have
to destroy half of Tel Aviv, the world will take that, too."

The British are too humane a people to send the Jews
of Europe to gas chambers as the Nazis did, but their government can be very cruel in an absent-minded and com-
placent way when the supposed needs of the Empire are
at stake. The British government doesn't intend to kill the
homeless Jews of Europe—it just wants to destroy their
hopes. But that amounts to the same thing in the end.
As one Jewish ex-Partisan said to me on shipboard, "The
Germans killed us. The British don't let us live."

The British are not playing a pro-Arab game. I have
heard the amused contempt with which British officials in
Cairo react to talk of Arab aspirations. The British are
trying to build an alliance with the Moslem upper classes

in the Middle East against the Soviet Union, and also against France and the United States. They want to keep the whole area under their control and they are prepared to sacrifice not only the Jews but the Christian minorities of the East in that program.

I am not making demagogic flourishes. I know how fearful the Christian minorities in Egypt, the Lebanon, and Iraq are of present British policy.

The Moslem upper class on the whole—with the exception of some far-sighted men—share with the British:

1. The phobia about the USSR.
2. Fear of unrest among the miserable Arab masses, and
3. Dislike for the modern ideas and methods brought to the ancient East by the returning Jews.

The British are shrewder than the pashas and the effendis. The British realize the need for development in the East. But development is now only possible with American capital, and they want to keep the Middle East as their private preserve. Development also would antagonize the reactionary ruling class elements who are the only allies the British can muster. One distinguished British oriental expert said to me, "If we urge social reform of the effendis, they will say 'what difference is there, then, between you and the Bolsheviks?'"

The clue to this aspect of British policy is that instead of asking for an American loan to develop the Jordan

Valley and similar water possibilities in Egypt, Syria, and Iraq, they are asking us to provide a $300,000,000 loan for the Arab potentates who rule those countries. There are no more corrupt rulers in the world today and the money will go straight into their private treasuries. This is the politics of *baksheesh*.

The British government wants the Middle East to remain an area of backwardness, a territory of "natives" and "native rulers" whom they can handle in the traditional way. They want Palestine to be their military base in the Middle East, and they offer freedom neither to the Arabs nor to the Jews. They who pride themselves on sportsmanship and gallantry are prepared to use overwhelming force —as they did when they ludicrously mobilized 5000 troops with tanks against the 160 villagers (50 of them children) in Sadoth Yam near Haifa.

I know the Jews of Palestine and I know how they must have chuckled at that unconscious tribute to their bravery and fighting power. The world will yet see that this is a struggle from which Britain will emerge with shame, but not with victory.

III

The exodus of Jews from Europe, of which I was an eye witness, is the greatest in the history of the Jewish people, greater than the migrations of the past out of Egypt and Spain. To tell its story properly one would need to be not a newspaper reporter, but an ancient Hebrew prophet. The journey was a journey for a Jeremiah. For it is a story which should be told as Parable and Warning.

The Jewish problem is a minor problem; Hitler left Bevin all too few. But what happens to them will be a portent. One need not believe in any divine retribution to see that the conditions which make it impossible for Jews to live in most of Central and Eastern Europe, and the conditions which block their aspiration for a return to their ancient homeland, are also the conditions which threaten mankind with new and quite possibly final disaster.

In that sense one need not be clairvoyant to see that history will exact a price for the treatment accorded the remnants of European Jewry. Unfortunately there is little comfort for the victims in apocalyptic perspectives.

In a sane and orderly world, the U.S.A., USSR, France, and Britain would join in an international development scheme for the Middle East and in a context of rising living standards provide ample room for the Jews in Palestine. I myself would like to see a bi-national Arab-Jewish state made of Palestine and Trans-Jordan, the whole to be part of a Middle Eastern Semitic Federation.

I would like to see a ten-year international trusteeship for Palestine in the course of which first through *consultative* and then using *representative* bodies, Jews and Arabs, Christians and Moslems would begin to work together as they do so successfully today in the half-Arab, half-Jewish municipality of Haifa.

After seeing Europe I am more than ever convinced

that Jews and Arabs can live together in peace. There is no such ill feeling in Palestine between Jew and Arab as exists in Czechoslovakia between Czech and Slovak, or in Yugoslavia between Croat and Serb.

I am also convinced that there isn't a chance of any such rational solution because the British don't want it, because it would set in motion a peaceful social revolution in the East, and because it would upset the potentates and pashas with whom the oil companies, American and British, do business.

I think the Jews must look to themselves and that they and those who are touched by their plight must put all their money and energies into the so-called illegal immigration. The only practical thing that can be done is to buy and man ships and with those ships to get the Jews out of Central and Eastern Europe.

What if the British catch most of the immigrants and send them to Cyprus? The answer is that Cyprus is only 180 miles from Palestine, that Jews are better off there than rotting morally in the DP camps, and that the job of the underground is to make their cruel blockade as costly and difficult as possible for the British.

This will be a crucial year for Jewry. There may be serious trouble in the camps, where morale is worse than ever. The British may widen offensive operations against Jewish settlements in Palestine. This is a war in which the lives and hopes of European Jewry and the accomplishments of the *Yishuv* in Palestine are at stake.

I believe that full support of the so-called illegal immigration is a moral obligation for world Jewry and a

Christian duty for its friends. I believe that the only hope lies in filling the waters of Palestine with so many illegal boats that the pressure on the British and the conscience of the world becomes unbearable.

And if those ships are illegal, so was the Boston Tea Party.

ACKNOWLEDGMENTS

I want to thank: Ralph Ingersoll, the editor, and John P. Lewis, the managing editor, of *PM,* for letting me make this trip and for the instinctive and characteristic humanity and sympathy they have displayed on this, as on every fundamental issue; Miss Viola Young, for some hard and devoted editorial work on the book; David Zucker, of Parish Press, for making possible an extraordinarily swift publication; and on this job of writing, as in all else, my wife.